Making Meaning™

Strategies That Build
Comprehension and Community

**DEVELOPMENTAL
STUDIES CENTER™**

Developmental Studies Center wishes to thank the following authors, agents, and publishers for their permission to reprint materials included in this program. Many people went out of their way to help us secure these rights and we are very grateful for their support. Every effort has been made to trace the ownership of copyrighted material and to make full acknowledgment of its use. If errors or omissions have occurred, they will be corrected in subsequent editions, provided that notification is submitted in writing to the publisher.

"A Nose for the Arts," *TIME For Kids* News Scoop Edition, December 14, 2002. Used with permission from TIME For Kids magazine. "Summer of the Shark," *TIME For Kids* News Scoop Edition, October 14, 2001. Used with permission from TIME For Kids Magazine. "Wild Rides," by Lev Grossman, *TIME For Kids* News Scoop Edition, May 10, 2002. Used with permission from TIME For Kids magazine.

All book covers reproduced in this manual by permission of the publishers.

Developmental Studies Center
2000 Embarcadero, Suite 305
Oakland, CA 94606-5300
(800) 666-7270, fax: (510) 464-3670
www.devstu.org

ISBN-13: 978-1-57621-403-9
ISBN-10: 1-57621-403-6

Printed in Canada

3 4 5 6 7 8 9 10

CONTENTS

Volume 2

Unit 5 ▶ Exploring Fiction

Unit 5 ▶ Exploring Fiction

During this unit, the students use wondering to understand a story. They continue to infer and make predictions, referring to the story to support their thinking. They relate the value of responsibility to their behavior. They also develop the group skills of sharing their thinking with one another and using a prompt to give reasons for their thinking. In Week 2, they have a check-in class meeting.

Week 1 ▶ *The Incredible Painting of Felix Clousseau*
by Jon Agee

The Ghost-Eye Tree
by Bill Martin, Jr. and John Archambault

Week 2 ▶ *Galimoto*
by Karen Lynn Williams

Week 3 ▶ *The Paper Crane*
by Molly Bang

Overview *of* Week 1

The Incredible Painting of Felix Clousseau*

by Jon Agee
(Farrar, Straus
& Giroux, 1988)

Synopsis
Unusual paintings make a painter famous.

This book is also used in Unit 6, Week 1.

The Ghost-Eye Tree

by Bill Martin, Jr.
and John Archambault,
Illustrated by Ted Rand
(Henry Holt, 1988)

Synopsis
A brother and sister are fearful of a tree they pass on their way to get a pail of milk on a dark, windy night.

Alternative Books

* *The Day of Ahmed's Secret*
  by Florence Parry Heide
  and Judith Heide Gilliland

* *If Nathan Were Here*
  by Mary Bahr

Comprehension Focus

* Students *wonder* to understand a story.

* Students make predictions and *infer*.

* Students refer to the story to support their thinking.

Social Development Focus

* Students relate the value of responsibility to their behavior.

* Students develop the group skills of sharing their thinking with one another and using a prompt to give reasons for their thinking.

Materials

- *The Incredible Painting of Felix Clousseau*

Day 1
Read-Aloud/Strategy Lesson

Lesson Purpose

Students:

▶ *Wonder* about a story read aloud.

▶ Refer to the story to support their thinking.

▶ Share their thinking and listen to one another.

▶ Begin working with a new partner.

About Wondering/Questioning

The purpose of this unit is to wonder about stories, building on the students' understanding of character and plot. *Wondering* is a strategy that good readers use to construct understanding. Students build this understanding through teacher modeling and making their own "I wonder" statements about the read-aloud book and their independent reading books.

▶ **PAIR STUDENTS AND GET READY TO WORK TOGETHER**

Randomly assign new partners and ask pairs to sit together. Remind the students that they have been talking about books and listening to one anothers' ideas. Doing this helps readers understand and enjoy books. First in pairs, then as a class, discuss:

Turn to Your Partner

Q *What are some things you would like your new partner to do to show that he or she is listening?*

2 INTRODUCE *THE INCREDIBLE PAINTING OF FELIX CLOUSSEAU* AND MODEL WONDERING

Show the cover of *The Incredible Painting of Felix Clousseau* and read the title and author's name aloud. Point to Felix Clousseau on the cover and explain that he is a painter who lives in Paris, France, and paints incredible—*incredible* means *unbelievable*—pictures.

Model wondering by thinking aloud about the title and the illustration on the cover. (For example, "I wonder what makes Felix's paintings incredible.") Ask:

Q *What do you wonder about this story?*

> **Students might say:**
>
> ❝ *I wonder what his paintings will be like."*
>
> ❝ *I wonder if it will be a funny story."*
>
> ❝ *I wonder why the people are waving to him."*

Explain that you will stop during the reading to have partners talk about what is happening in the story and what they are wondering about.

▶ READ ALOUD AND STOP AND WONDER

Read the story aloud, showing the illustrations, and stopping as described below.

Suggested Vocabulary

armor: metal covering for the body, used as a defense (p. 8)

outrageous: shocking (p. 10)

stunned: shocked (p. 13)

hailed: greeted enthusiastically (p. 16)

commissioned: ordered (p. 16)

baroness: noblewoman (p. 18)

chaos: complete confusion (p. 21)

seized: taken by force (p. 25)

notorious: well-known, usually for something bad (p. 26)

ferocious: very fierce (p. 28)

Read pages 5–13. Stop after:

> [p. 13] "The judges were stunned."

Ask:

Q *What has happened so far?*

Teacher Note

If the students have difficulty generating "I wonder" statements, model several like those in the "Students might say" note. Be ready to continue modeling during the reading until the students seem comfortable generating "I wonder" statements on their own.

Have one or two students share. Then ask:

Q *What do you wonder about the story at this point?*

Have the students use "Turn to Your Partner" to discuss the question. Have two or three volunteers share with the class. Ask the students to begin their sharing with the prompt "I wonder…."

> **Students might say:**
>
> ❝ *I wonder if he'll win the prize."*
>
> ❝ *I wonder if someone is behind the painting."*
>
> ❝ *I wonder if he has magic paint."*

Without stopping to discuss the statements, reread the sentence on page 13 and continue reading to the next stop. Repeat this process at each stop:

> [p. 25] "Clousseau's paintings were seized…all except one."
>
> [p. 28] "The crown was saved."

Continue reading to the end of the story. Ask:

Q *What do you wonder about the ending of the story?*

Have the students use "Turn to Your Partner" to discuss the question. Have two or three volunteers share with the class.

> **Students might say:**
>
> ❝ *I wonder who painted him since he came out of the picture."*
>
> ❝ *I wonder if the whole town was a painting."*
>
> ❝ *I wonder if he might be magic because he came out of the picture."*

Turn to Your Partner

▶ DISCUSS THE STORY AS A CLASS

Use "Turn to Your Partner" to have the students talk about what they are still wondering about the story. Then facilitate a whole-class discussion. Ask:

Q *What is this story about?*

Q *What do you think of this story? Did you like it? Why? Why not?*

Tell the students you will use wondering again in the next lesson.

5▶ REFLECT ON GROUP WORK

Facilitate a brief discussion about how the students showed their partners that they were listening.

Individualized Daily Reading

6▶ DOCUMENT IDR CONFERENCES

Have the students read books at their reading level independently for 20 minutes.

Use the "IDR Conference Notes" record sheet to conduct and document individual conferences.

At the end of independent reading, have partners discuss their books. Circulate as the pairs talk and ask questions such as:

Q *What is happening in the story?*

Q *What are you wondering about the story?*

Extension

7▶ REREAD THE STORY

Reread *The Incredible Painting of Felix Clousseau* aloud. As a class, discuss any additional things the students wonder about the story.

Materials

• *The Ghost-Eye Tree*

• Scratch paper and a pencil

Day 2
Read-Aloud/Strategy Practice

Lesson Purpose

Students:

▶ *Wonder* about a story.

▶ Share their thinking with one another.

▶ REVIEW WONDERING AND WORKING TOGETHER

Have partners sit together. Remind them that in the last lesson they heard *The Incredible Painting of Felix Clousseau* and talked to their partner about what they wondered as they listened to the story. Explain that today they will listen to another story and talk to their partner about what they wonder as they listen. Ask:

Q *How does listening to your partner's ideas help you wonder?*

Q *What can you do to make sure you are both offering ideas?*

Teacher Note

At the end of today's lesson, you will create a chart with several of the students'"I wonder" statements in preparation for tomorrow's lesson. Jot down some of the statements you hear the students making on a sheet of scratch paper. You will select among these statements when you create the chart. (See the "Teacher Note" on page 172.)

▶ INTRODUCE *THE GHOST-EYE TREE*

Show the cover of *The Ghost-Eye Tree* and read the title and names of the authors and illustrator aloud. Tell the students that this is a story about a walk a brother and sister take to get a bucket of milk. Explain that you will read the story aloud and stop during the reading to have partners talk about what they are wondering about the story. Ask:

Q *Often, one of the first things a reader does is wonder about the title and the illustration on the cover of the book. What do you wonder about the title* The Ghost-Eye Tree?

Have the students use "Turn to Your Partner" to discuss the question. • • • • •   **Turn to Your Partner**

> **Students might say:**
>
> ❝ I wonder why the tree is called the ghost-eye tree."
>
> ❝ I wonder if it is a magical tree."

Have two or three volunteers share their ideas with the class.

▶ READ *THE GHOST-EYE TREE* ALOUD AND STOP AND WONDER

Read *The Ghost-Eye Tree* aloud, showing the illustrations, and stopping as described below.

Suggested Vocabulary

dreaded: feared (p. 3)

muttering: speaking in a quiet, unclear way (p. 11)

Read pages 3–15, and stop after:

> [p. 15] "Help me carry the milk."

Ask:

Q *What has happened so far?*

Have the students use "Turn to Your Partner" to discuss the question. Then ask:

Q *What do you wonder about the story at this point?*

Have the students use "Turn to Your Partner" to discuss this question. Have two or three volunteers share what they wonder with the class. Remind them to start with the prompt "I wonder…."

> **Teacher Note**
>
> To maintain the flow of the lesson, have only two or three students share at each stop. Accept the students' "I wonder" statements without discussion. Hearing others' statements gives students examples of things they might wonder about as they hear a story.

Without discussing the "I wonder" statements, reread the last sentence on page 15 and continue reading. Follow the same procedure at the next stop:

> [p. 22] "We set the bucket down…flopped on the ground… gasping… for breath…"

Reread the last sentence on page 22, and continue reading to the end of the book. Ask:

Q *What are you still wondering?*

> **Students might say:**
>
> ❝ *I wonder if the sister is also scared."*
>
> ❝ *I wonder why the sister says 'here's your dumb hat.'"*
>
> ❝ *I wonder if the ghost-eye tree is a real tree."*

> **Teacher Note**
>
> If the students wonder about things that are unconnected to the story, help them to connect their questions to the text by asking, "What in the book makes you wonder that?"

4▸ DISCUSS THE STORY AS A CLASS

Facilitate a brief class discussion, using questions such as:

Q *Why do you think they were afraid of the tree?*

Q *Why do you think the sister went back for her brother's hat?*

Q *How does this story make you feel? What parts made you feel [excited]?*

5▸ REFLECT ON WORKING TOGETHER

Help the students think about how they worked together today. Ask:

Q *How did you and your partner do making sure that you both shared ideas? What could you do differently next time to make it go better?*

> **Teacher Note**
>
> In preparation for the Day 3 lesson, select four or five of the students' "I wonder" statements that you recorded on scratch paper today, and write them on a sheet of chart paper entitled "I Wonder About *The Ghost-Eye Tree*." If possible, select both statements that are addressed in the story and statements that are not addressed.

Individualized Daily Reading

▶ DOCUMENT IDR CONFERENCES

Have the students read independently for 20 minutes.

Use the "IDR Conference Notes" record sheet to conduct and document individual conferences.

At the end of independent reading, have the students talk with their partner about their book. Circulate as the students discuss their books and ask questions such as:

Q *What is happening in the story?*

Q *What are you wondering about the story?*

Materials

- *The Ghost-Eye Tree*

- "I Wonder About *The Ghost-Eye Tree*" chart, prepared ahead (see the "Teacher Note" on page 172)

- *Assessment Record Book*

- *Student Book,* IDR Journal section

Day 3
Strategy Lesson

Lesson Purpose

Students:

▶ Refer to the story to support their thinking.

▶ Learn a prompt to give reasons for their thinking.

▶ 1 INTRODUCE AND MODEL GIVING REASONS FOR YOUR THINKING

Have partners sit together. Explain that today you will reread *The Ghost-Eye Tree* and they will revisit some of the things they wondered about the story yesterday.

Explain that during today's discussion you would like the students to focus on giving a reason for their thinking whenever they share. Write the prompt "I think _____, because _____" where everyone can see it, and briefly model using the prompt. (For example, "I think giving a reason for my thinking is a good idea, because it helps everyone understand my thinking.")

Encourage the students to use the prompt when they share today, and tell them that you will check in with them at the end of the lesson.

▶ 2 REVIEW "I WONDER" STATEMENTS

Refer to the "I Wonder About *The Ghost-Eye Tree*" chart and read the "I wonder" statements aloud. Remind the students that these are some of the things they wondered as they heard the story. Ask the students to keep these questions in mind as you reread the story. Tell them that after you read, partners will talk about whether or not the "I wonder" statements on the chart are discussed in the story.

▶ REREAD *THE GHOST-EYE TREE*

Reread the story aloud, showing the illustrations as you read.

▶ DISCUSS "I WONDER" STATEMENTS

Read an "I wonder" statement from the chart. Ask:

Q *Is this answered in the book? How?*

Have the students use "Turn to Your Partner" to discuss
the question.

· · · · · · · **Turn to Your Partner**

Class Comprehension Assessment

As partners discuss the "I wonder" statements, circulate among
them and ask yourself:

Q *Are the students using the "I wonder" statements to discuss
the book?*

Q *Are they using evidence from the text to support their thinking?*

Record your observations on page 18 of the *Assessment Record Book*.

Have a few volunteers share their thinking with the class. Remind
the students to use the prompt "I think _____, because
_____" as they talk.

Use the same procedure to discuss the other "I wonder" statements. During this discussion, explain that it is normal for some
"I wonder" statements to be addressed in a story, while others
might not be. Whether they are addressed or not, wondering
during reading helps readers be more active thinkers as they read.

▶ **5 REFLECT ON GIVING REASONS FOR YOUR THINKING**

Briefly discuss how the students did using the prompt "I think _____, because _____" as they talked today. Encourage them to continue to use the prompt whenever they are sharing their thinking during the school day.

Individualized Daily Reading

▶ **6 DOCUMENT IDR CONFERENCES/
HAVE THE STUDENTS WRITE IN THEIR "IDR JOURNAL"**

Ask the students to notice what they wonder as they read today. Explain that at the end of IDR they will write about what they like about their book .

Have the students read independently for 20 minutes.

Use the "IDR Conference Notes" record sheet to conduct and document individual conferences.

At the end of independent reading, have the students write in their "IDR Journal" about what they like about their book. You might want to write the prompt "I like this book because…." where everyone can see it.

Exploring Fiction

Overview
of Week 2

Galimoto
by Karen Lynn Williams,
Illustrated by
Catherine Stock
(Mulberry, 1991)

Synopsis
A boy searches for
wires to make
a toy car, called
a galimoto.

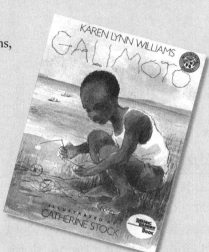

Alternative Books

* *Elisabeth* by Claire A. Nivola
* *Our Gracie Aunt*
  by Jacqueline Woodson

Comprehension Focus

* Students *wonder* to understand a story.
* Students make predictions and *infer*.
* Students refer to the text to support their thinking.

Social Development Focus

* Students relate the value of responsibility to their behavior.
* Students develop the group skills of sharing their thinking with one another and using a prompt to give reasons for their thinking.
* Students have a check-in class meeting.

▶ **Do Ahead**

* Prepare to model wondering in independent reading (see Day 3, Step 2 on page 183).

Materials

- *Galimoto*
- Scratch paper and a pencil

Day 1
Read-Aloud/Strategy Lesson

Lesson Purpose

Students:

▶ *Wonder* about a story.

▶ Share their thinking with one another.

▶ GET READY TO WORK TOGETHER

Ask partners to sit together. Remind them that they have been listening to stories and talking to their partner and the class about what they wonder about the stories. Explain that today they will listen to a story and wonder about it before, during, and after the reading. Remind them that they will be responsible for thinking on their own and explaining their thinking to their partner and the class.

▶ INTRODUCE *GALIMOTO*

Show the cover of *Galimoto* and read the title and names of the author and illustrator aloud. Ask:

Q   *What do you wonder about the story?*

Have two or three volunteers share their ideas with the class.

> **Students might say:**
>
> ❝ *I wonder if galimoto is a thing or a boy.* ❞
>
> ❝ *I wonder what galimoto means.* ❞

Explain that *Galimoto* is a story about a boy named Kondi who walks around his town collecting things. He meets and talks to several people— Ufulu, Kondi's brother; Gift, Kondi's friend; and Munde, Gift's sister. Write the characters' names on the board.

Teacher Note

As you did last week, you will create a chart with several of the students' "I wonder" statements in preparation for this week's Day 2 lesson. During today's lesson, jot down some of the students' statements on a sheet of scratch paper. You will select among these statements when you create the chart. (See the "Teacher Note" on page 180.)

Explain that you will read the story aloud, stopping in the middle and at the end to have partners talk about what they are wondering.

▶ READ *GALIMOTO* ALOUD AND STOP AND WONDER

Read *Galimoto* aloud, showing the illustrations as you read, and stopping as described below.

Suggested Vocabulary

flour mill: a building containing machinery for grinding grain into flour (p. 12)

maize: corn (p. 12)

spokes: thin metal rods that connect the rim of the wheel to the hub (p. 18)

Stop after:

> [p. 10] "'Take the wires.'"

Ask:

Q *What has happened so far?*

Have the students use "Turn to Your Partner" to discuss the question. Then ask:

Q *What do you wonder about the story so far?*

Have the students use "Turn to Your Partner" to discuss the question. Have two or three volunteers share what they wonder with the class. Without stopping to discuss the questions, reread the last paragraph on page 10 and continue reading. Follow the same procedure at the next two stops:

> [p. 21] "'Thief, thief,' they chanted, pointing at Kondi."

> [p. 28] "'Perhaps tomorrow I shall make my galimoto into an ambulance or an airplane or a helicopter.'"

Turn to Your Partner

Turn to Your Partner • • • • •

Teacher Note

In preparation for the Day 2 lesson, select four or five of the students' "I wonder" statements that you recorded on scratch paper today, and write them on a sheet of chart paper entitled "I Wonder About *Galimoto*." If possible, select both statements that are addressed in the story and statements that are not addressed.

4 DISCUSS THE STORY IN PAIRS AND AS A CLASS

First in pairs, then as a class, discuss:

Q *What are some problems in this story? How are they solved?*

Q *Kondi likes to make galimotos. If you were to build a galimoto, what would you like to build?*

Remind the students to use the prompt. "I think _____, because _____."

Tell the students that they will revisit the story again tomorrow.

Individualized Daily Reading

5 DOCUMENT IDR CONFERENCES/HAVE THE STUDENTS DISCUSS "I WONDER" STATEMENTS

Have the students read books at appropriate reading levels independently for 20 minutes.

Use the "IDR Conference Notes" record sheet to conduct and document individual conferences.

At the end of independent reading, have partners discuss their books. Circulate as the students talk and ask questions such as:

Q *What is happening in the story?*

Q *What are you wondering about the story?*

Have a few volunteers share their ideas with the class, and model writing two or three of their "I wonder" statements where everyone can see them. Tell the students that they will write their own statements during the next IDR period.

Day 2
Strategy Lesson

Lesson Purpose

Students:

▸ Refer to the story to support their thinking.

▸ Share their thinking with one another.

▸ Use a prompt to give reasons for their thinking.

Materials

- *Galimoto*

- "I Wonder About *Galimoto*" chart, prepared ahead (see the "Teacher Note" on page 180)

- *Student Book,* IDR Journal section

▶ REVIEW THE "I WONDER" STATEMENTS

Have partners sit together. Show the cover of *Galimoto* and remind the students that they wondered about the book in the previous lesson. Read the statements on the "I Wonder About *Galimoto*" chart aloud, and explain that these are some of the things they wondered about. Explain that as they listen to the story again you would like them to think about whether or not these "I wonder" statements are addressed in the story.

▶ REREAD *GALIMOTO*

Reread *Galimoto* aloud, without stopping.

▶ DISCUSS THE "I WONDER" STATEMENTS

Read an "I wonder" statement from the chart. Ask:

Q *Is this answered in the book? How?*

Have the students use "Turn to Your Partner" to discuss the questions, and then have a few students share their thinking with the class. Remind the students to use the prompt "I think _____, because _____" as they talk.

Turn to Your Partner

Use the same procedure to discuss the other "I wonder" statements. During this discussion, remind the students that some of their "I wonder" statements may be addressed in the story, while others might not. Whether or not the questions are addressed, wondering helps readers be more active thinkers as they read.

▶ REFLECT ON GIVING REASONS FOR THINKING

Briefly discuss how the students did using the prompt "I think _____, because _____" as they talked today. Encourage them to continue to use the prompt whenever they share their thinking during the school day.

Individualized Daily Reading

▶ DOCUMENT IDR CONFERENCES/ HAVE THE STUDENTS WRITE AN "I WONDER" STATEMENT IN THEIR "IDR JOURNAL"

Explain that at the end of IDR, the students will write an "I wonder" statement about their reading in their "IDR Journal." Ask them to notice what they wonder about their book as they read today.

Have the students read books at appropriate reading levels independently for up to 20 minutes.

At the end of independent reading, model an "I wonder" statement by reading part of a story aloud, thinking aloud about something you wonder, and writing an "I wonder" statement on the chalkboard where everyone can see it. Ask the students to write their own statements in their "IDR Journal," starting with the words "I wonder."

Day 3
Independent Strategy Practice

Lesson Purpose

Students:

▶ Stop and wonder about stories read independently.

▶ Share their thinking with one another.

▶ Have a check-in class meeting.

Materials

- Narrative text to model wondering in independent reading (see Step 2)

- Books at appropriate levels for independent reading

- Small self-stick notes for each student

- "Class Meeting Ground Rules" chart

- "Our Class Norms" chart

- Scratch paper and a pencil

- *Assessment Record Book*

1 REVIEW WONDERING

Have partners sit together. Remind the students that this week they heard *Galimoto* read aloud, and stopped and wondered to help them better understand and discuss the story. Explain that today the students will wonder about stories they read independently.

2 MODEL WONDERING WITH INDEPENDENT READING

Model wondering when reading independently by using a narrative text of your own and a self-stick note. Examine the book cover and read a few sentences aloud. Then wonder aloud about a question that comes to mind. Write a question mark on your self-stick note and place it in your book at the place where you thought of the question. Distribute the self-stick notes, and have the students write question marks on the notes. Explain that they will use the notes to mark places in their books where they wonder about something or where a question comes to mind.

3 READ INDEPENDENTLY

Have the students read independently. After five minutes, stop the class to have partners share what they have wondered about so far. Then have the students read for another five minutes.

Teacher Note

As the students work, circulate and notice whether they are marking places where they have questions.

Turn to Your Partner • • • • •

4 DISCUSS THE INDEPENDENT READING

At the end of independent reading time, use "Turn to Your Partner" to have the students talk about what they wondered about their books.

Class Comprehension Assessment

Circulate among the students and ask yourself:

Q *Are the students wondering about characters and events in their story?*

Record your observations on page 19 of the *Assessment Record Book*.

Have several volunteers share what they wondered with the class. Probe the students' thinking by asking:

Q *What in the story made you wonder about that?*

Q *What are you still wondering about?*

Explain that during the next lesson the students will have more opportunities to wonder about stories.

5 HAVE A BRIEF CHECK-IN CLASS MEETING

Tell the students they will have a brief check-in class meeting, and have them move with their partner into a circle. Review the "Class Meeting Ground Rules" and "Our Class Norms" charts. Explain that the topic of today's meeting will be ways to improve class discussions. First in pairs, and then as a class, discuss:

Q *What are we doing well during our class discussions?*

Q *What things do we want to focus on to improve during our class discussions?*

Class Meeting Ground Rules

- One person talks at a time.

Our Class Norms

- We will talk nicely to one another.

Remind the students to use the prompt "I think _____, because _____" as they share. Jot down a few notes for yourself to use during future class discussions to remind the students of what they agreed to work on.

Briefly discuss how the students did following the "Class Meeting Ground Rules" and adjourn the meeting.

Teacher Note

In the time period following a class meeting, it is important to hold the students accountable for things they agreed to work on. Use your notes to regularly remind the students and to check in with them about how they are doing.

Exploring Fiction
[Wondering/Questioning]

Overview
of Week 3

e Paper Crane

Molly Bang
ulberry, 1985)

nopsis

popular roadside
taurant loses its
tomers when a
ghway is built
replace the old road.
hen a stranger gives the restaurant
ner a special gift in exchange for his kindness,
fortune is changed.

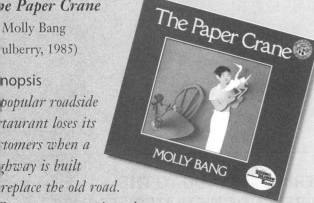

Alternative Books

· *Sylvester and the Magic Pebble*
  by William Steig

· *Spinky Sulks* by William Steig

Comprehension Focus

· Students *wonder* to understand a story.

· Students make predictions and *infer*.

· Students refer to the text to support
  their thinking.

Social Development Focus

· Students relate the value of responsibility to
  their behavior.

· Students develop the group skills of sharing
  their thinking with one another and using a
  prompt to give reasons for their thinking.

Materials

- *The Paper Crane*
- "Reading Comprehension Strategies" chart
- Scratch paper and a pencil

Reading Comprehension Strategies
- making connections

Day 1
Read-Aloud

Lesson Purpose

Students:

▶ *Wonder* about a story.

▶ Share their thinking with one another.

▶ Use a prompt to give reasons for their thinking.

▶ DISCUSS WONDERING AND ADD TO THE "READING COMPREHENSION STRATEGIES" CHART

Have partners sit together. Refer to the "Reading Comprehension Strategies" chart and remind the students that they have been listening to stories and talking to their partner about what they wondered as they listened. Explain that wondering about what you are reading is a strategy that readers use to make sense of stories. Write *wondering* on the chart, and point out that this is another strategy the students will use this year to make sense of what they read.

Explain that today you will read a story aloud and they will have another chance to wonder about the story before, during, and after the reading.

▶ INTRODUCE *THE PAPER CRANE*

Show the cover of *The Paper Crane* and read the title and author's name. Read the summary on the back cover aloud. Ask:

Q *What do you wonder about this story?*

Have two or three volunteers share their ideas with the class.

> ***Students might say:***
>
> ❝ *I wonder what the magic in the paper crane is."*
>
> ❝ *I wonder if the crane is going to come alive."*
>
> ❝ *I wonder who the stranger is."*

Explain that you will stop in the middle and at the end of the story to have partners talk about what they wonder.

▶ READ *THE PAPER CRANE* ALOUD AND STOP AND WONDER

Read *The Paper Crane* aloud, showing the illustrations, and stopping as described below.

Suggested Vocabulary

host: a person who welcomes you into their home or shop (p. 11)

crane: a type of bird (p. 12)

overjoyed: very happy (p. 23)

ELL Vocabulary

English Language Learners may benefit from discussing additional vocabulary, including:

highway: a main road (p. 6; refer to the illustration)

company: guests or visitors (p. 19)

Stop after:

[p. 12] "With these words the stranger left."

Use "Turn to Your Partner" to discuss:

Turn to Your Partner

Q *What do you wonder about the story so far?*

Teacher Note

At the end of today's lesson, you will create a chart with several of the students'"I wonder" statements in preparation for tomorrow's lesson. Jot down some of the students' statements on a sheet of scratch paper. Select among these statements when you create the chart. (See the "Teacher Note" on page 191.)

Turn to Your Partner ▪ ▪ ▪ ▪ ▪

Have two or three volunteers share what they wonder. Without stopping to discuss the statements, reread the last sentence on page 12 and continue reading to the next stop. Repeat this process at each stop:

[p. 23] "The owner knew him at once and was overjoyed."

[p. 28] "He climbed on the back of the crane, and they flew out of the door and away."

[p. 31] "But neither the stranger nor the dancing crane has ever been seen again."

Students might say:

❝ I wonder if the stranger is going to give the owner another magical gift."

❝ I wonder why the man flew away with the crane."

❝ I wonder if the man goes where people need help."

4▶ DISCUSS THE STORY

First in pairs, then as a class, discuss the following questions. (You may want to substitute some of the students'"I wonder" statements for the questions.)

Remind the students to give reasons for their thinking.

Q *Why do you think the stranger gave the restaurant owner such a wonderful gift?*

Q *Why do you think the stranger took back the crane?*

5▶ REFLECT ON WORKING TOGETHER

Facilitate a brief discussion about how the students worked together today. Ask:

Q *How does hearing others share what they wonder help you think more about the story?*

Students might say:

“ *Sometimes when I hear someone talk about part of the story, it reminds me of what happened in the story."*

“ *When I hear someone wonder about something in the story, I start to wonder about it too."*

Tell the students that in the next lesson, they will listen to the story again and discuss whether what they wonder is addressed in the story.

Individualized Daily Reading

6 REVIEW THE "READING COMPREHENSION STRATEGIES" CHART/READ INDEPENDENTLY

Refer to the "Reading Comprehension Strategies" chart and review the strategies on it. Encourage the students to use these strategies to make sense of their reading.

Have the students read books at appropriate reading levels independently for 20 minutes.

As the students read, circulate among them and talk to individual students about their reading. Ask questions such as:

Q *What is your book about? What's happening in your book right now?*

Q *Are you wondering about anything so far? If so, what?*

Q *What do you know about the main character? Why do you think that?*

Q *What strategies are you using to help you understand the story?*

Teacher Note

In preparation for the Day 2 lesson, select four or five of the students' "I wonder" statements that you recorded on scratch paper today, and write these on a sheet of chart paper entitled "I Wonder About *The Paper Crane*." If possible, select both statements that are addressed in the story and statements that are not addressed.

At the end of independent reading, have the students share what they read as a whole class. Ask questions such as:

Q *What is happening in your story?*

Q *What is a reading comprehension strategy on the chart you used when reading today? How did it help you understand your story?*

Day 2
Strategy Practice

Lesson Purpose

Students:

▸ Refer to the story to support their thinking.

▸ Share their thinking with one another.

▸ Use a prompt to give reasons for their thinking.

Materials

....

• *The Paper Crane*

• "I Wonder About *The Paper Crane*" chart, prepared ahead (see the "Teacher Note" on page 191)

• *Student Book,* IDR Journal section

❶ REVIEW "I WONDER" STATEMENTS

Have partners sit together. Show the cover of *The Paper Crane* and remind the students that in the previous lesson they wondered before, during, and after the read-aloud. Explain that today they will listen to the story again and think about whether what they wondered is addressed in the story.

Read the "I wonder" statements on the "I Wonder About *The Paper Crane*" chart aloud. Explain that these are some of the things the students wondered about when they heard the story. Ask the students to keep these ideas in mind as you reread the story. Explain that at the end of the rereading, partners will discuss whether the story talks about what they wondered.

❷ REREAD *THE PAPER CRANE*

Reread the story aloud without stopping.

❸ DISCUSS THE "I WONDER" STATEMENTS

Read an "I wonder" statement from the chart. Ask:

Q *Is this answered in the book? How?*

Turn to Your Partner ● ● ● ● ●

Have the students use "Turn to Your Partner" to discuss the question, then have a few students share their thinking with the class. Remind the students to use the prompt "I think _____, because _____" as they talk.

Use the same procedure to discuss the other "I wonder" statements.

◢ REFLECT ON REREADING

Review the day's lesson. Remind the students that rereading is an important technique that readers use to think more deeply about a story. Point out that when they heard *The Paper Crane* again and discussed whether what they wondered was explained in the story, they were thinking more deeply about the story.

Ask:

Q *What did you think about during the second reading of* The Paper Crane *that you didn't think about during the first reading?*

Encourage the students to use rereading when they read independently to help them think more deeply about the story.

Individualized Daily Reading

◢ DOCUMENT IDR CONFERENCES/ HAVE THE STUDENTS WRITE AN "I WONDER" STATEMENT IN THEIR "IDR JOURNAL"

Ask the students to notice what they wonder as they read today. Explain that at the end of IDR they will write an "I wonder" sentence in their "IDR Journal."

Have the students read independently for 20 minutes.

Use the "IDR Conference Notes" record sheet to conduct and document individual conferences.

At the end of IDR, ask the students to write one or two "I wonder" statements in their "IDR Journal."

Extensions

⑥ MAKE PAPER CRANES

Read *Sadako and the Thousand Paper Cranes* by Eleanor Coerr. Discuss how the paper crane became a symbol of peace. Model making a paper crane, and have each student make one.

⑦ JOIN A THOUSAND CRANES PEACE PROJECT

As an ongoing project, have the class make a thousand cranes as an expression of hope for world peace. You may send the cranes to any of several peace organizations that you can find on the Internet.

Teacher Note

The following books contain instructions for making paper cranes: *Origami Classroom* or *Easy Origami* by Dokuotei Nakano, or *Spread Your Wings and Fly* by Mary Chloe Saunders. You can also visit your library for books or http://teachervision.com/lesson-plans/lesson-4295.html for instructions.

If making paper cranes is too difficult for your second-graders, you may want to demonstrate folding the crane or show a folded crane. Then, model folding simpler figures for the students to make.

Day 3
Independent Strategy Practice

Lesson Purpose

Students:

▶ *Wonder* about stories read independently.

▶ Refer to the stories to support their thinking.

▶ Explain their thinking.

▶ REVIEW WONDERING

Remind the students that this week they heard *The Paper Crane* and thought about whether or not their "I wonder" statements were explained in the story.

▶ PREPARE TO WONDER DURING INDEPENDENT READING

Explain that today the students will wonder about stories they read independently. Review using self-stick notes to mark places where they wonder. Distribute the self-stick notes, and have the students use them to mark places in their books where they wonder about something or where a question comes to mind.

▶ READ INDEPENDENTLY

Have the students read independently for up to 15 minutes. Circulate and ask the students what they are reading and what they wonder. Stop the class at five-minute intervals to talk with their partner about their wondering.

Class Comprehension Assessment

Cirlcuate and ask yourself:

Q *Are the students wondering as they read?*

Q *Are their questions relevant to the text?*

Record your observations on page 20 of the *Assessment Record Book*.

4▶ DISCUSS THE INDEPENDENT READING

First in pairs, then as a class, discuss:

Q *As you read today, what did you wonder about?*

Q *What was happening in the story when you wondered that?*

Q *Did the book answer what you wondered? How?*

Review with the students what they have learned in this unit. Remind them that wondering about stories helps readers better understand what they are reading. Tell the students to note questions they have or what they wonder about during their reading throughout the day.

5▶ REFLECT ON WORKING TOGETHER

Ask pairs to discuss:

Q *How has your partner helped you to become a better reader?*

Ask a few volunteers to share their ideas with the class.

····· **Turn to Your Partner**

Teacher Note

This is the last week of Unit 5. If you feel your students need more experience with wondering before you move on to the next unit, you may want to repeat this week's Days 1 and 2 lessons with an alternative book. Alternative books are listed on this week's Overview page.

You will reassign partners for Unit 6.

Individual Comprehension Assessment

Before continuing with Unit 6, take this opportunity to assess individual students' progress in using wondering to understand text. Please refer to pages 36–37 in the *Assessment Record Book* for instructions.

Social Skills Assessment

Take this opportunity to assess your students' social development using the "Social Skills Assessment" record sheet on pages 4–5 of the *Assessment Record Book*.

This assessment will occur again after Unit 7.

Unit 6 ▶ Exploring Nonfiction

Unit 6 ▶ Exploring Nonfiction

During this unit, the students explore the difference between fiction and nonfiction text and identify what they learn from nonfiction text. They use schema and wondering/ questioning to make sense of texts. They also informally explore features of expository text. Socially, they develop the group skill of contributing ideas that are different from other people's ideas. They continue to relate the value of responsibility to their behavior, and they have a class meeting to discuss how they are following the class norms.

Week 1 ▶ *The Tale of Peter Rabbit*
by Beatrix Potter

Beatrix Potter
by Alexandra Wallner

Week 2 ▶ *The Art Lesson*
by Tomie dePaola

"Draw, Draw, Draw": A Short Biography of Tomie dePaola

Week 3 ▶ *It Could Still Be a Worm*
by Allan Fowler

Plants that Eat Animals
by Allan Fowler

Week 4 ▶ *Fishes (A True Story)*
by Melissa Stewart

Week 5 ▶ *POP! A Book About Bubbles*
by Kimberly Brubaker Bradley

Overview *of* Week 1

The Tale of Peter Rabbit
Beatrix Potter
(Frederick Warne, 1987)

Synopsis
This classic tale describes Peter Rabbit's adventures in Mr. McGregor's garden.

Beatrix Potter
Alexandra Wallner
(Holiday House, 1995)

Synopsis
This book describes the life of Beatrix Potter and how the tale of Peter Rabbit became a story that children still enjoy today.

Alternative Books

• *Author: A True Story* by Helen Lester

• *Monet* by Mike Venezia

Comprehension Focus

• Students explore the difference between fiction and nonfiction texts.

• Students identify what they learn from text.

• Students *use wondering/questioning* to make sense of text.

Social Development Focus

• Students relate the value of responsibility to their behavior.

• Students develop the group skill of contributing ideas that are different from other people's ideas.

▶ Do Ahead

• Collect nonfiction texts that the students can examine and read independently (see "About Exploring Nonfiction" on page 207).

• Prepare the chart for self-monitoring during IDR (see Day 1 IDR on page 205).

Materials

- *The Tale of Peter Rabbit*
- Scratch paper and a pencil

Teacher Note

The edition of *The Tale of Peter Rabbit* suggested for this week is a new version of the original 1902 edition. It is very small and the students will have difficulty seeing the illustrations during the read-aloud. Before and after today's lesson, give the students opportunities to look at the illustrations on their own.

The students will also hear a biography of Beatrix Potter this week. If possible, collect other books by Beatrix Potter for them to read independently.

Teacher Note

If the students had a chance to see the book before the read-aloud, you might want to read without showing the illustrations.

Day 1
Read-Aloud

Lesson Purpose

Students:

▶ Hear and discuss a story.

▶ Share their thinking.

---

❶ PAIR STUDENTS AND GET READY TO WORK TOGETHER

Randomly assign partners and have them sit together. Explain that for the next five weeks they will work with this partner.

Tell the students that they will be talking with their partner about books they hear read aloud. Ask:

Q *What did you do the last time you worked with a partner that will help you work with your new partner?*

❷ INTRODUCE *THE TALE OF PETER RABBIT*

Show the cover of *The Tale of Peter Rabbit* and explain that it was the first story Beatrix Potter wrote and illustrated. She wrote it and many similar books 100 years ago, and children still enjoy reading them. Explain that you will read a story about Beatrix Potter's life in the next lesson.

Explain that you will stop during the reading of *The Tale of Peter Rabbit* to have partners talk about the story.

❸ READ *THE TALE OF PETER RABBIT* ALOUD

Read the story aloud, showing the illustrations, and stopping as described on the next page.

mischief: playful behavior that may bother or harm others (p. 13)

implore him to exert himself: begged him to try and get up (p. 33)

sieve: a container with lots of small holes in it (p. 34; refer to the illustration on p. 35)

hoe: a gardening tool with a long handle and a thin blade (p. 49)

fortnight: two weeks (p. 54)

Stop after:

> [p. 10] "'…he was put in a pie by Mrs. McGregor.'"

Ask:

Q *What does Mrs. Rabbit mean when she says that their father had an accident?*

Have a few students share with the class. Reread page 10 and continue reading to the next stopping point:

> [p. 18] "But Peter who was very naughty, ran straight away to Mr. McGregor's garden, and squeezed under the gate!"

Ask:

Q *What has happened so far, and what do you think will happen next?*

Have the students use "Turn to Your Partner" to discuss the question. Without stopping to share as a class, reread page 18 and continue reading to the next stop. Follow this procedure at the next three stopping points:

· · · · · · **Turn to Your Partner**

> [p. 30] "It was a blue jacket with brass buttons, quite new."

> [p. 41] "He went back to his work."

> [p. 49] "His back was turned towards Peter, and beyond him was the gate!"

Continue reading to the end of the book.

4 ▶ DISCUSS THE STORY

As a class, discuss:

Q *What part of the story did you like best?*

As the students respond, reread the parts of the story they mention and show the illustrations.

5 ▶ WONDER ABOUT BEATRIX POTTER

Remind the students that in the next lesson they will hear a true story about Beatrix Potter's life. Ask:

Q *After hearing* The Tale of Peter Rabbit *and seeing the illustrations, what are some things you wonder about Beatrix Potter? What would you like to find out about her?*

> **Students might say:**
>
> ❝ *I wonder if she enjoyed writing children's books."*
>
> ❝ *I wonder if she had a pet rabbit."*
>
> ❝ *I wonder if she only wrote books about animals."*
>
> ❝ *I wonder if she was married and had children of her own."*

Tell the students that some of their questions might be addressed in the book about Beatrix Potter they will hear in the next lesson.

Teacher Note

Record a few of the students' "I wonder" statements on scratch paper. In particular, record questions that might be addressed in Beatrix Potter's biography.

---

6 ▶ REFLECT ON WORKING TOGETHER

Facilitate a brief discussion about how partners worked together. Ask questions such as:

Q *What worked well for you and your new partner today?*

Q *What do you want to keep working on?*

Tell the students that they will have more opportunities to work with their partner.

Individualized Daily Reading

▶ TEACH SELF-MONITORING

Before the students read independently, explain that today you will stop them periodically during IDR to have them think about how well they are understanding their own reading. Tell them that good readers pause while reading to think about what they are reading and how well they are understanding. Direct their attention to the following questions, which you have written on chart paper labeled "Thinking About My Reading."

- What is happening in my story right now?

- Does the reading make sense?

- How many words on the page I just read are new to me? How many words don't I know?

- Would it be better to continue reading this book or get a new book?

Read each of the charted questions aloud. Explain that these questions will help them know whether their book is right for them. Explain that when you stop them you would like them to think about each of these questions quietly before continuing to read. When they realize that they are not understanding, they need to reread. If they don't understand after the second reading, they may need to get a new book.

Have the students read independently for up to 20 minutes. Stop them at ten-minute intervals, read the questions on the chart aloud, and have them monitor their comprehension by thinking about the questions.

As they read, circulate among them and ask individual students to read a selection aloud for you and tell you what it is about. Use the questions on the chart to help struggling students practice monitoring their own comprehension.

At the end of independent reading, have the students talk about how the questions on the chart helped them monitor their own comprehension.

Day 2
Read-Aloud/Strategy Lesson

Lesson Purpose

Students:

▶ Compare fiction and nonfiction.

▶ Identify what they learn from a nonfiction text.

▶ *Wonder* about the text.

▶ Share their thinking.

About Exploring Nonfiction

The purpose of this unit is to introduce the students to nonfiction text and help them make sense of nonfiction using the reading comprehension strategies they have learned in earlier units. These strategies include *making connections* to information the students already know, *wondering* or *asking questions* about topics they read about, and *visualizing* what authors describe. The unit's primary goal is for the students to use comprehension strategies to make sense of what they read, rather than to recall the many facts presented in the books.

In this unit the students informally compare nonfiction and fiction and explore some of the features of expository text, such as photographs, chapter titles, tables of contents, glossaries, and indexes.

If possible, provide a variety of narrative nonfiction (biographies and autobiographies) and expository text for the students to read independently. Expository texts include books and magazines like *Ask, Discover, Ranger Rick,* and *Scholastic News.*

▶ INTRODUCE NONFICTION

Have partners sit together. Remind them that yesterday they heard *The Tale of Peter Rabbit.* Explain that this story is called *fiction* because it has make-believe characters, places, and things that happen. Write *fiction: make-believe stories* on the board. Direct the

Materials
....

- *Beatrix Potter*

- "I wonder" statements you recorded on scratch paper on Day 1

- Scratch paper and a pencil

- Variety of fiction and nonfiction books

- "Thinking About My Reading" chart

Teacher Note
Display a few nonfiction and fiction texts where all the students can see them. Select texts that at least some of your students have read or heard.

students' attention to some of the other fiction books you displayed and point out that these books are also fiction.

Explain that during the coming weeks the students will hear and read books about real people, animals, and plants. Explain that these books are called *nonfiction*. Write *nonfiction: books about real people, places, and things* on the board. Direct the students' attention to the nonfiction books you displayed, briefly describing each one. (For example, "*Reptiles* is a nonfiction book that gives lots of information about snakes, such as where they live and what they eat.")

2▶ INTRODUCE *BEATRIX POTTER* AND BUILD BACKGROUND KNOWLEDGE

Show the cover of *Beatrix Potter* and read the title and author's name aloud. Explain that this is a true story about Beatrix Potter, the author of *The Tale of Peter Rabbit*. Point out that a nonfiction book that tells the story of a person's life is called a *biography*.

Explain that Beatrix was born in England around 150 years ago. Beatrix loved science, animals, and drawing. She often drew pictures and wrote about animals.

Read aloud some of the "I wonder" statements that you jotted down at the end of the previous lesson. Ask the students to listen for answers to their questions.

3▶ READ *BEATRIX POTTER* ALOUD WITH BRIEF SECTION INTRODUCTIONS

Explain that today you will read the first part of the book aloud and that you will stop during the reading to have partners talk about what they are learning about Beatrix's life.

Teacher Note

This week's read-aloud contains a lot of factual information that the students might have difficulty following. To support them, you will introduce each section briefly before you read it. This will help focus the students' listening on the main ideas discussed in that section.

---

governesses: women who take care of other people's children (p. 4)

fond: liking something very much (p. 6)

boarding school: a school at which the students live (p. 10)

companion: a person who accompanies another (p. 10)

bronchitis: an illness of the throat and lungs (p. 12)

rheumatic fever: a children's disease (p. 12)

ELL Note

English Language Learners may benefit from viewing accompanying illustrations before hearing the text. They may also benefit from explanation of additional vocabulary.

Explain that the first part of the book describes Beatrix's and her brother Bertram's lives as children. Start reading on page 4, showing the illustrations as you read. Stop after:

[p. 6] "Beatrix was especially fond of two pet mice named Hunca Munca and Appley Dapply, and a rabbit named Peter."

Ask:

Q *What did you learn about Beatrix as a child?*

Teacher Note
You might want to reread pages 4–6 before discussing the question.

Have the students use "Turn to Your Partner" to discuss the question; then ask a few volunteers to share with the class.

Explain that the next part of the book tells about Beatrix's interest in painting. Ask the students to listen for what they learn about this. Reread the last sentence before the stop and continue reading to the next stop:

[p. 9] "Her years of practice made her an excellent painter."

Ask:

Q *What did you learn about Beatrix Potter's interest in painting?*

Have the students use "Turn to Your Partner" to discuss the question; then ask a few volunteers to share with the class.

Turn to Your Partner

Explain that the next part of the book tells about Beatrix's good friend Annie Carter, and how Beatrix came to write *The Tale of Peter Rabbit*. Reread the last sentence on page 9 and continue reading to the next stop:

> [p. 15] "She didn't think about writing other stories because she was more interested in making drawings and keeping notes on science."

Ask:

Q *What have you learned about how Beatrix got the idea for The Tale of Peter Rabbit?*

Have two or three pairs share what they learned.

Briefly paraphrase page 16. Read the last paragraph on page 16 and continue to read to the next stopping point:

> [p. 21] "The book was very popular and made a lot of money for her."

Ask:

Q *What did you learn from the part of the story I just read?*

Teacher Note
Page 16 of the book contains information that is not directly related to how Beatrix Potter wrote and published *The Tale of Peter Rabbit*. To maintain the students' focus on how the author wrote her book, we suggest that you briefly paraphrase page 16.

4▸ DISCUSS WHAT THE STUDENTS LEARNED AND WONDER
Remind the students that today they learned about Beatrix Potter's life from her childhood to the age of 36. Ask:

Q *What did you learn about Beatrix Potter that surprised you?*

> ***Students might say:***
>
> ❝ *I was surprised that she was alone a lot and didn't have many friends."*
>
> ❝ *I think it is funny that her parents hired a friend for her."*
>
> ❝ *I was surprised that her parents did not let her live alone."*

Remind the students that *wondering*, or *questioning*, is a strategy that can help them think about what they are reading.

Ask:

Q *Based on what you know so far about Beatrix Potter, what do you wonder about her?*

Tell the students that some of their questions might be answered in the next lesson, when they hear the rest of *Beatrix Potter.*

Teacher Note

Record a few of the students' "I wonder" statements on scratch paper. In particular, record questions that might be addressed in the last part of the book.

▷ REFLECT ON WORKING TOGETHER

Briefly discuss how partners worked together. Point out ways you noticed the students contributing to their partner conversations and listening to one another.

Individualized Daily Reading

▷ PRACTICE SELF-MONITORING

Have the students read nonfiction independently for up to 20 minutes.

Stop them at ten-minute intervals and have them monitor their comprehension by thinking about the questions on the "Thinking About My Reading" chart.

Thinking About My Reading
- What is happening in my story right now?

As they read, circulate among them and ask individual students to read a selection aloud to you and tell you what it is about. Use the questions on the chart to help struggling students practice monitoring their own comprehension.

At the end of independent reading, have the students talk about how the questions on the chart helped them monitor their own comprehension.

Materials

- *Beatrix Potter*
- Your jotted "I wonder" statements from Days 1 and 2
- *Student Book,* IDR Journal section
- *Assessment Record Book*

Day 3
Read-Aloud/Strategy Lesson

Lesson Purpose

Students:

▶ Identify what they learn from a nonfiction text.

▶ *Wonder* about the text.

▶ Contribute ideas that are different from other people's ideas.

▶ INTRODUCE AND BRIEFLY MODEL CONTRIBUTING DIFFERENT IDEAS

Have partners sit together. Review that this year they have learned several skills to help them work with their partner, such as explaining their thinking and listening carefully to each other.

Explain that today the students will learn a new skill: contributing ideas that are different from their partner's ideas. Point out that this skill is especially useful when reading nonfiction books with lots of information, such as *Beatrix Potter.* If each partner contributes different ideas, then together the pair can remember more information.

Choose a volunteer to act as your partner. Show the cover of *Beatrix Potter* and ask:

Q *What do you remember about Beatrix Potter from the first part of the book?*

Listen as your partner talks; then model contributing a different idea. (For example, "You remembered that Beatrix was lonely as a child because she didn't have any friends. In addition to what you said, I learned that she first wrote about Peter Rabbit in a letter to Noel, who was Annie's son.")

Turn to Your Partner • • • •

Ask partners to briefly practice the skill by taking turns telling each other different things they remember from the first part of the book.

❷ READ THE REST OF *BEATRIX POTTER* ALOUD WITH BRIEF SECTION INTRODUCTIONS

Explain that you will read the rest of the book aloud today, and the students will learn about Beatrix's life after she became famous for writing *The Tale of Peter Rabbit*.

Suggested Vocabulary

tales: stories (p. 22)

proposed: asked her to marry him (p. 25)

disapproved: didn't think it was a good idea (p. 26)

museums: places where interesting objects of art, history, or science are displayed (p. 28)

tourists: people who travel and visit places for pleasure (p. 28)

private: quiet, keeping to oneself (p. 30)

modest: not boastful (p. 30)

ELL Note

English Language Learners might benefit from viewing accompanying illustrations before hearing the text. They might also need explanation for additional vocabulary words.

Remind the students that at the end of the first day's reading, Beatrix had just become famous and wealthy because of her book, *The Tale of Peter Rabbit*. Explain that the next part of the book tells about Beatrix's time at Hilltop Farm in the countryside of England. Reread page 21 and continue reading to the following stopping point:

[p. 22] "Finally, Beatrix was doing what she wanted and was happy."

Ask:

Q *What have you learned about Beatrix in this part of the story?*

Have the students use "Turn to Your Partner" to discuss the question. Remind them to share different ideas. Then ask a few volunteers to share their ideas with the class.

Turn to Your Partner

Explain that the last part of the book talks about Beatrix's marriage. Reread page 22 and continue reading to the next stopping point:

[p. 26] "Her eyesight was getting weak, and she preferred spending her time with her animals and farming."

Teacher Note

If you want to shorten this reading, you might paraphrase rather than read pages 24 and 25.

Turn to Your Partner • • • • •

First in pairs, then as a class, discuss:

Q *What new information have you learned about Beatrix Potter?*

Have two or three pairs share what they learned. Reread the last sentence on page 26 and continue reading to the end of the book.

Class Comprehension Assessment

As the students share, ask yourself:

Q *Have the students learned new things about Beatrix Potter from the reading?*

Q *Are partners contributing different ideas?*

Record your observations on page 21 of the *Assessment Record Book*.

3▶ DISCUSS THE BOOK AND WHAT THE STUDENTS WONDER

Facilitate a brief whole-class discussion about what the students learned and what they wonder. Ask questions such as:

Q *In what ways did Beatrix use her own life to help her write her stories?*

Q *What was the most surprising or interesting thing that you learned about Beatrix Potter?*

Read aloud and discuss one or two of the "I wonder" statements that you jotted down on Days 1 and 2 to connect the students' questions with information in the text. Point out that they could read other books or magazines or use the Internet to find out more about Beatrix Potter.

▶4 REFLECT ON CONTRIBUTING DIFFERENT IDEAS

Briefly discuss how the students did contributing ideas that were different from their partner's ideas. Ask questions such as:

Q *How did you and your partner do contributing different ideas?*

Q *Were you able to remember more of the book together by contributing different ideas? Give us an example.*

Explain that partners will have more opportunities to practice contributing different ideas in the next lesson.

Individualized Daily Reading

▶5 PRACTICE SELF-MONITORING/ WRITE IN THE "IDR JOURNAL"

Have the students read nonfiction independently for up to 20 minutes.

As they read, circulate among them and ask individual students to read a selection aloud for you. Use the questions on the "Thinking About My Reading" chart to help struggling students practice monitoring their own comprehension.

At the end of independent reading, have the students write in their "IDR Journal" about their reading.

Extensions

▶6 READ OTHER TALES BY BEATRIX POTTER

Read other stories by Beatrix Potter, and have the students discuss the tales and their connections to her life. (For example, she had a pet bunny named Bounce, and she wrote a story about a bunny.)

▷ LEARN MORE ABOUT BEATRIX POTTER

Read other stories about Beatrix Potter. Biographies of Potter for young readers are: *Beatrix Potter* by Elizabeth Buchan, *My Dear Noel: The Story of a Letter from Beatrix Potter* by Jane Johnson, *Beatrix Potter (Tell Me More)* by John Malam, and *Beatrix Potter (Lives and Times)* by Jayne Woodhouse.

Overview *of* Week 2

The Art Lesson
by Tomie dePaola
(PaperStar, 1999)

Synopsis
This autobiographical
tale recounts Tomie
dePaola's early love
of drawing.

Alternative Books

· *Now One Foot, Now the Other*
  by Tomie dePaola

· *The Baby Sister* by Tomie dePaola

Comprehension Focus

· Students identify what they learn from
  nonfiction text.

· Students *use wondering/questioning* to
  make sense of text.

Social Development Focus

· Students relate the value of responsibility
  to their behavior.

· Students develop the group skill of
  contributing ideas that are different from
  other people's ideas.

· Students have a class meeting to discuss
  how they are following the class norms.

▸ **Do Ahead**

· Collect books written or illustrated by
  Tomie dePaola (including other autobiographical stories) for the students to
  read independently.

· Prepare a chart with the title "What We
  Wonder About Tomie dePaola" (see Day 2,
  Step 2 on page 222).

Materials

- *The Art Lesson*

- Variety of books written and/or illustrated by Tomie dePaola

Day 1
Read-Aloud

Lesson Purpose

Students:

▶ Identify what they learn from a nonfiction text.

▶ *Wonder* about and *make personal connections* to a text.

▶ Contribute ideas that are different from other people's ideas.

Teacher Note

In this lesson, the students will hear a story about Tomie dePaola's childhood interest in art. To introduce the lesson, display a few of his books where all the students can see them. Try to select books that are familiar to some of your students. If possible, read a couple of the books prior to this lesson.

1 ▶ REVIEW BIOGRAPHICAL NONFICTION AND BUILD BACKGROUND KNOWLEDGE

Have partners sit together. Review that last week the students listened to a biography of Beatrix Potter, and that a biography is a nonfiction story that tells about someone's life. Explain that today they will hear a story called *The Art Lesson,* by Tomie dePaola. Tomie based the story on his own childhood.

Refer to the books you have displayed and explain that these are books that have been written and/or illustrated by Tomie dePaola. Briefly show a few and ask the students whether they are familiar with any of them.

2 ▶ INTRODUCE *THE ART LESSON*

Show the cover of *The Art Lesson* and explain that it is a story about a boy who loves to draw. Read the first paragraph on the back cover aloud.

Explain that you will stop during the reading to have partners talk about what they are learning and wondering.

❸ READ *THE ART LESSON* ALOUD AND WONDER

Read *The Art Lesson* aloud, showing the illustrations, and stopping as described below.

> **Suggested Vocabulary**
>
> **barber shop:** a place to get a haircut (p. 9)
>
> **carpenters:** workers who build and repair wooden structures (p. 14)
>
> **school property:** materials that belong to the school (p. 22)
>
> **paper monitor:** child in charge of passing out paper in the classroom (p. 25)

Stop after:

> [p. 14] "But, when the painters came, his dad said, 'That's it, Tommy. No more drawing on the walls.'"

Ask:

Q *What have you learned about Tommy so far?*

Have two or three students share their ideas with the class. Then ask:

Q *What are you wondering at this point in the story?*

Have the students use "Turn to Your Partner" to discuss the question, reminding them to try to come up with questions that are different from their partner's questions. Have one or two students share with the class. Reread the last sentence and continue reading to the next stopping point:

· · · · · **Turn to Your Partner**

> [p. 18] "…and she always carried a big box of thick colored chalks."

Ask:

Q *Now what are you wondering?*

Turn to Your Partner ● ● ● ● ●

Have the students use "Turn to Your Partner" to discuss the question. Have one or two students share with the class. Reread page 18 and continue reading to the next stopping point:

[p. 23] "And Joe was right. They only got ONE piece of paper."

Ask:

Q How do you think Tommy feels at this point? What do you think will happen next?

Have the students use "Turn to Your Partner" to discuss the questions. Have one or two students share their thinking with the class. Reread the last sentence on page 23 and continue reading to the end of the book.

❹ DISCUSS THE STORY AND MAKE CONNECTIONS

Facilitate a whole-class discussion using questions such as:

Q What part of the story did you like best?

Q What was Tommy's problem when he went to school? How was it solved?

Q Have you ever felt or acted like Tommy does in this story?

As the students respond, reread the passages they mention and show the corresponding illustrations.

❺ REFLECT ON WORKING TOGETHER

Facilitate a brief discussion about how partners worked together. Ask:

Q How did you and your partner do contributing ideas that were different from each other's? Give us some examples.

Tell the students that they will hear a short biography of Tomie dePaola in the next lesson. Invite them to look at and read the other books by Tomie dePaola on their own.

Individualized Daily Reading

▶ PRACTICE SELF-MONITORING/ DOCUMENT IDR CONFERENCES

Have the students read nonfiction books independently for up to 20 minutes. Ask the students to use the questions on the "Thinking About My Reading" chart.

Use the "IDR Conference Notes" record sheet to conduct and document individual conferences.

At the end of independent reading, have the students share their reading with the class. Ask questions such as:

Q *What do you like about what you read?*

Q *What surprised you in your reading?*

Extension

▶ READ OTHER AUTOBIOGRAPHICAL STORIES BY TOMIE DEPAOLA

Read other autobiographical stories by Tomie dePaola and have the students discuss the stories and make personal connections. Some other stories based on his life are *Nana Upstairs & Nana Downstairs, The Baby Sister, Tom,* and *Now One Foot, Now the Other.*

Materials

- *The Art Lesson*

- *"Draw, Draw, Draw"* (see pages 226–230)

- "What We Wonder About Tomie dePaola" chart and a marker

Day 2
Read-Aloud/Strategy Lesson

Lesson Purpose

Students:

▶ Identify what they learn from a nonfiction text.

▶ *Wonder* about the text.

▶ Contribute ideas that are different from other people's ideas.

▶ REVIEW *THE ART LESSON*

Have partners sit together. Show the cover of *The Art Lesson* and remind the students that Tomie dePaola based this story on his own childhood. Leaf through the pages of the book and show the illustrations. Ask:

Q *What did we learn about the character Tommy in this book?*

Have a few students share. Remind them to contribute different ideas.

▶ INTRODUCE "DRAW, DRAW, DRAW" AND WONDER

Explain that today they will hear a short biography of Tomie dePaola called "Draw, Draw, Draw." Remind the students that a biography is nonfiction—it is a true story about a person's life. Ask:

Q *What are some things you wonder about Tomie dePaola?*

Think, Pair, Share

Have the students use "Think, Pair, Share" to discuss the question. Have a few students share what they are wondering, and record their questions or "I wonder" statements on the "What We Wonder About Tomie dePaola" chart. Ask the students to think about these questions as you read the biography.

Explain that you will stop during the reading to have partners talk about what they are learning. This biography does not have illustrations so they can use their imaginations to visualize as you read.

Teacher Note

If possible, show the students a photograph of Tomie dePaola. The book *Tomie dePaola: His Art & His Stories* by Barbara Elleman contains several photographs.

❸ READ "DRAW, DRAW, DRAW" ALOUD

Read "Draw, Draw, Draw" aloud, stopping as described below.

Suggested Vocabulary

appears: shows up

family legend: family story passed down from one generation to the next

was determined: had his mind made up

deep fried: cooked in fat, like french fries

tap dancing: dancing with special shoes that make clicking noises

performing onstage: dancing or acting on a stage

hire: give a person a job

reveals: tells

fabulous: wonderful

Read the first five paragraphs and stop after:

"…and continued until he grew up, often performing onstage."

Ask:

Q *What did you learn about Tomie as a child?*

Have the students use "Turn to Your Partner" to discuss the question. Then ask a few volunteers to share their ideas.

Turn to Your Partner

Class Comprehension Assessment

As the students contribute to this discussion, ask yourself:

Q *Are the students' ideas connected to the text?*

Q *Are partners contributing different ideas?*

Record your observations on page 22 of the *Assessment Record Book*.

Reread the last sentence before the stop and continue reading. Stop after:

> "One was Arnold Lobel, who wrote and illustrated the *Frog and Toad* series."

Ask:

Q *What did you learn about Tomie in the part that I just read?*

Turn to Your Partner ● ● ● ● ●

Have the students use "Turn to Your Partner" to discuss the question. Then ask a few volunteers to share their ideas. Reread the last sentence and continue reading to the end of the biography.

At the end of the reading, turn to the last page of *The Art Lesson* and point out the symbol of the white bird with a pink heart. Tell the students that they might look for this symbol when they read other stories by Tomie dePaola.

▶ DISCUSS WHAT THE STUDENTS LEARNED AND WONDER

Facilitate a brief whole-class discussion about what the students learned and wondered.

Ask:

Q (Refer to the "What We Wonder About Tomie dePaola" chart.) *What did we learn about Tomie dePaola that could help us answer some of the questions we had?*

Q *What did you learn about Tomie dePaola that surprised you?*

▶ REFLECT ON WORKING TOGETHER

Briefly discuss how partners worked together. Point out ways you noticed students contributing ideas that were different from their partner's.

Individualized Daily Reading

▶ PRACTICE SELF-MONITORING/ DOCUMENT IDR CONFERENCES

Have the students read nonfiction books independently for up to 20 minutes. Ask them to use the questions on the "Thinking About My Reading" chart.

Use the "IDR Conference Notes" record sheet to conduct and document individual conferences.

At the end of independent reading, have the students share their reading with the class. Ask questions such as:

Q *What do you like about what you read?*

Q *What surprised you in your reading?*

Extension

▶ LEARN MORE ABOUT TOMIE DEPAOLA

Use the questions on the "What We Wonder About Tomie dePaola" chart to learn more about him. *Tomie dePaola: His Art & His Stories* by Barbara Elleman contains additional information, photographs of Tomie and his family, and examples of his illustrations and paintings.

"Draw, Draw, Draw": A Short Biography of Tomie dePaola

Tomie dePaola was born on September 15, 1934, in Meriden, Connecticut, where his father worked as a barber. His parents named him Thomas Anthony dePaola after his two grandfathers. His Irish grandpa, Tom Downey, was a hero of Tomie's. He appears in many of the author's books, including <u>Now One Step, Now the Other</u>, and <u>Tom</u>. His Italian grandpa, Antonio dePaola, died before Tomie was born.

Why does Tomie spell his name the way he does? A family legend says that before he was born, Tomie's mother joked to her cousin that she thought the active baby might grow up to be a dancer. Her cousin, Morton Downey, a famous singer, knew that Mrs. dePaola was planning to name her son Thomas. According to the story, Morton said that if little Tommy was going to be famous, he would have to spell his name "differently." So Tomie did, and he is—famous, that is.

"Draw, Draw, Draw": A Short Biography of Tomie dePaola

Tomie was the second child in a family of four children. Maureen, who was born after Tomie, was his favorite. His book <u>The Baby Sister</u> tells how happy Tomie was when she was born. The two loved making puppets together and putting on shows for their family. The grown-up brother and sister are still close friends.

DePaola describes himself as a stubborn little boy. He was determined to learn to cook and insisted on creating his own recipes. He says, "I found out that flour and water and ketchup, deep fried, didn't taste very good, but I had to discover that for myself."

Besides doing artwork, Tomie loved reading, putting on shows, and dancing, just as his mother predicted. He began taking tap dancing lessons at age five and continued until he grew up, often performing onstage.

As a boy, Tomie had many great teachers. The ones he loved best were Beulah Bowers, the art teacher he describes in <u>The Art Lesson</u>, his fifth grade teacher, Rose

"Draw, Draw, Draw": A Short Biography of Tomie dePaola

Mulligan, who read aloud to the class every day, and Miss Leah, his tap dancing teacher.

When he was in fourth grade, Tomie sent one of his pictures to Walt Disney, the famous cartoonist who created Mickey Mouse. Tomie was sure that Mr. Disney would see what a good artist he was and hire him to help make Disney cartoons. Disney sent the boy's picture back with a letter of advice. He told Tomie to keep his early artwork and practice. Tomie paid attention to this advice. He drew all the time. DePaola says that when children write to him today he takes their letters very seriously, because he knows how important good advice can be.

Tomie's twin cousins, Franny and Fuffy McLaughlin, went to an art college called Pratt Institute. After high school, Tomie went there, too. For him, art school was "heaven on earth." His teachers encouraged him to "keep your eyes open and draw, draw, draw." Some of Tomie's friends at Pratt also went on to create popular

"Draw, Draw, Draw": A Short Biography of Tomie dePaola

children's books. One was Arnold Lobel, who wrote and illustrated the <u>Frog and Toad</u> series.

Even though he practiced all the time, it took many years for Tomie to get his first job as a book illustrator, drawing the pictures for a nonfiction book called <u>Sound</u>, written by Lisa Miller.

Soon Tomie began writing his own books instead of just illustrating other writers' work. Many of his books are based on his own life. In <u>The Art Lesson</u> he describes his beloved art teacher, Mrs. Bowers, and the box of 64 crayons that he received as a birthday gift. <u>Nana Upstairs & Nana Downstairs</u> tells about Tomie's Irish grandma and great-grandma. <u>Oliver Button Is a Sissy</u> reveals that as a boy Tomie was terrible at sports, though he was a fabulous tap dancer.

Tomie dePaola also writes and illustrates religious stories, folktales, and made-up stories with funny characters such as Strega Nona, Big Anthony, and Bill and Pete, pals who happen to be a crocodile and a bird. "All of my characters seem to be parts of me," says dePaola.

Today Tomie dePaola lives in New London, New Hampshire. To make an art studio, he fixed up a large 200-year-old barn. Though he has no children, he has many nieces and nephews. He also has four dogs named Madison, Markus, Morgan, and Moffat.

The symbol for dePaola's company, Whitebird Inc., is a little white bird with a pink heart on its chest. This symbol appears in many of his books. When Tomie dePaola signs his name, he often adds a little pink heart to his signature.

Day 3
Class Meeting

Materials

- Space for the class to sit in a circle

- "Class Meeting Ground Rules" chart

- "Our Class Norms" chart

- "Thinking About My Reading" chart

- *Student Book,* IDR Journal section

Lesson Purpose

Students:

▶ Participate in a class meeting.

▶ Analyze the ways they have been living by the class norms.

▶ Share their thinking with one another.

▶ GATHER FOR A CLASS MEETING

Tell the students that they are going to have a class meeting today to check in on how they are living by the class norms to create a safe and caring environment. Have them move to the circle, with partners sitting together, and briefly review the ground rules.

Class Meeting Ground Rules
- One person talks at a time.

▶ REFLECT ON THE CLASS NORMS AND READING COMMUNITY

Refer to the "Our Class Norms" chart. As you read each norm aloud, ask the students to think about how they have lived by the norm over the past few weeks to help create a caring and safe reading community.

Our Class Norms
- We will talk nicely to one another.

After a few moments of individual reflection, use the following questions to facilitate a whole-class discussion:

Q *What is one norm that you've lived by? How has this helped our reading community?*

Q *What are some examples you've seen of your classmates living by the norms?*

Q   *Are you feeling safe and respected in our reading community? If yes, why? If not, what suggestion do you have for creating a safer and more respectful community?*

Turn to Your Partner • • • • •

During the discussion, ask the students not to use names when giving examples and to avoid blaming or accusing others. Use "Turn to Your Partner" as needed during this discussion to increase participation, especially if you are hearing from only a few students. You can also use "Turn to Your Partner" if many students want to speak at the same time.

Explain that you would like the students to think of one norm they will try extra hard to live by in the coming days. Tell them that you will check in with them again about how they are living by the norms and contributing to the reading community.

▶ ADJOURN THE CLASS MEETING

Refer to the "Class Meeting Ground Rules" chart and ask:

Q   *How do you think we did using the ground rules during today's class meeting?*

Q   *What do you think we still need to work on?*

Have the students briefly review the procedure for returning to their desks and adjourn the meeting.

Individualized Daily Reading

▶ REVIEW SELF-MONITORING/ WRITE IN THE "IDR JOURNAL"

Refer to the "Thinking About My Reading" chart and review the questions. Remind the students that it is important to check their reading comprehension as they are reading.

Have the students read for up to 20 minutes. As the students read, circulate among them and ask questions such as:

Q *What is your book about?*

Q *What are you learning about [frogs] from this book? What do you wonder about [frogs]?*

Q *If you don't understand what you are reading, what do you do? How is this helpful?*

At the end of independent reading, have the students write about what they learned in their "IDR Journal."

Overview
of Week 3

Could Still Be a Worm
Allan Fowler
Children's Press, 1996)

ynopsis
*his book is a simple
troduction to the
rthworm, roundworm,
tworm, and other
nds of worms.*

lants that Eat Animals
Allan Fowler
Children's Press, 2001)

ynopsis
*variety of carnivorous
ants, including the
enus's-flytrap, sundew,
tcher plant, and
adderwort are described.*

Alternative Books

- *It Could Still Be a Butterfly*
  by Allan Fowler

- *It Could Still Be a Flower*
  by Allan Fowler

Comprehension Focus

- Students *use schema* to help them understand nonfiction texts.

- Students identify what they learn from the texts.

- Students *use wondering/questioning* to make sense of the texts.

- Students informally *explore expository text features.*

Social Development Focus

- Students relate the value of responsibility to their behavior.

- Students develop the group skill of contributing ideas that are different from other people's ideas.

Day 1
Read-Aloud

Lesson Purpose

Students:

▶ Use what they already know to help them understand a nonfiction text.

▶ Identify what they learn from the text.

▶ *Use wondering/questioning* to make sense of the text.

▶ Contribute ideas that are different from other people's ideas.

▶ REVIEW BIOGRAPHIES AND INTRODUCE ANOTHER KIND OF NONFICTION

Have partners sit together. Remind the students that in previous lessons they listened to two biographies, or nonfiction stories about people's lives. The biographies told the stories of Beatrix Potter and Tomie dePaola.

Tell the students that today they will listen to another type of nonfiction that gives true information about topics such as animals, plants, places, and weather. For example, the nonfiction book you will read to them today gives information about worms.

▶ INTRODUCE *IT COULD STILL BE A WORM* AND WONDER

Show the cover of *It Could Still Be a Worm* and read the title and author's name aloud. Point out that since nonfiction books tell about real things, many are illustrated with photographs rather than drawings or paintings. Show a few of the photos, such as the sea worm photo on the cover and the earthworm photo on page 3. Briefly discuss:

Q *What do you think you know about worms?*

Q *Based on what you know, what do you wonder about them?*

Tell the students that you will stop several times during the read-aloud so partners can talk about what they are learning from the book. After you have read the book, they will share with the class what they learned and what they wonder about worms.

▶ READ ALOUD WITH BRIEF SECTION INTRODUCTIONS

Read *It Could Still Be a Worm* aloud, showing the photographs and stopping as described below.

Suggested Vocabulary

segments: parts or sections (p. 4)
bristles: stiff hairs (p. 5)
automobile: car (p. 8)
attract the fish: make the fish come (p. 13)
dull: not bright (p. 16)
crops: plants (p. 23)
moisture: wetness (p. 25)
wormcasts: worms' solid waste (p. 26)

Tell the students that the first part you will read tells about the sizes of different worms. Begin reading and stop after:

[p. 8]   "…like this giant Australian earthworm."

Ask:

Q *What did you learn about different worms' sizes?*

Have the students use "Turn to Your Partner" to discuss the question. Remind them to try to contribute ideas that are different from their partner's ideas.

After a minute, tell the students that the next part you will read tells about places where worms can live. Resume reading and stop after:

[p. 15]   "…a sea worm or a ribbon worm."

Teacher Note

Make sure the students understand that they will not share with the class at each stop. This maintains the flow of the text and cultivates the habit of relying on a partner—rather than the teacher or the whole class—to confirm and support the students' thinking.

Teacher Note

Today's read-aloud contains a lot of factual information which the students might have difficulty following. To support them, you will briefly introduce each section before you read it. This will help to focus the students' listening on the main ideas discussed in that section.

Teacher Note

You may need to read each passage twice before having partners discuss it.

Turn to Your Partner

Turn to Your Partner • • • • •

Have the students use "Turn to Your Partner" to discuss:

Q *What did you learn about places where worms can live?*

After a minute, tell the students that the next part tells what different worms look like. Resume reading and stop after:

[p. 20] "…young insects that haven't yet grown into their adult form."

Have the students use "Turn to Your Partner" to discuss:

Q *What did you find out about what worms can look like?*

After a minute, tell the students that the last part of the book tells some ways that worms can be harmful and helpful. Resume reading and stop after:

[p. 29] "…and still be a worm."

Have the students use "Turn to Your Partner" to discuss:

Q *How can worms be harmful and helpful to people, plants, and animals?*

▶ DISCUSS WHAT THE STUDENTS LEARNED AND WONDER

Show pages 30–31, the "Words You Know" section. Briefly point out that some nonfiction books include sections like this one that use photos or pictures to explain the meanings of words from the book. Use the photos shown to help the students recall what they learned from *It Could Still Be a Worm*.

Use the following questions to facilitate a whole-class discussion. Remind the students to try to contribute ideas that are different from those other people contribute. Ask:

Q *What did you learn about worms from this book that interested or surprised you?*

Q *What are you still wondering about worms?*

> **Students might say:**
>
> ❝ *I wonder if worms have eyes."*
>
> ❝ *I wonder how worms can be cut in half and still live."*
>
> ❝ *I wonder if worms can be harmful to other worms."*

Tell the students that they will hear another nonfiction book tomorrow.

Teacher Note

If necessary, probe the students' thinking with questions such as:

Q *How long or short can worms be?*

Q *Where can worms live?*

Q *Why are worms important to people, animals, and plants?*

▷ **REFLECT ON WORKING TOGETHER**

Ask, and discuss as a whole class:

Q *Did you and your partner remember different information from the book? How did that help your learning today?*

Tell the students that they will hear another nonfiction book tomorrow.

Individualized Daily Reading

▷ **MODEL PREVIEWING A TEXT BEFORE READING**

Remind the students that they have been practicing pausing to check how well they are understanding what they are reading. Another strategy that good readers use is to look at the cover, read the information on the back of the book, and preview the book by looking through the pages to help them get acquainted with the book before reading it. Model previewing a book for the students. Tell them looking over a nonfiction book before reading is especially helpful.

Ask the students to take the time to look over their book today before starting to read today even if it is a book they have already begun.

Have them read nonfiction independently for up to 20 minutes.

As they read, circulate and ask individual students questions such as:

Q *What did you notice about your book when you looked it over before you started to read? How was this helpful to you?*

At the end of independent reading, have the students share their reading with their partner.

Extension

▷ REVISIT *VISUALIZING*

Several passages in *It Could Still Be a Worm* are good ones for the students to visualize. Remind the students that *visualization* is one of the strategies readers use to help them understand what they are reading. Have them close their eyes and picture, or visualize, the following passages:

[p. 8] "Or a worm could be longer than an automobile and still be a worm—like this giant Australian earthworm."

[p. 10] "A small farm might have more worms than a big city has people."

[p. 19] "If they [earthworms] are cut into two or more pieces, each piece can live by itself as a whole worm."

After reading each of these passages, have the students discuss their mental images, first in pairs, then as a class. Then ask the students to select one of the passages and draw a picture of the images they created. Have partners compare their drawings. As a class, discuss how visualizing helped them better understand the text.

Day 2
Read-Aloud/Strategy Lesson

Materials

- *Plants that Eat Animals*
- *Student Book,* IDR Journal section

Lesson Purpose

Students:

▶ Identify what they learn from a nonfiction text.

▶ *Use wondering/questioning* to make sense of the text.

▶ Contribute ideas that are different from other people's ideas.

▶ REVIEW THE PREVIOUS LESSON

Have partners sit together. Review that in the previous lesson, the students listened to a nonfiction book about worms and talked with their partner and the class about what they learned and wondered. Explain that today they will listen to a book that gives information about unusual kinds of plants.

▶ INTRODUCE *PLANTS THAT EAT ANIMALS*

Show the cover of *Plants that Eat Animals* and read the title and author's name aloud. Ask:

Q   *When you hear the title of this book,* Plants that Eat Animals, *what do you wonder about?*

> **Students might say:**
>
> ❝ *I wonder what kinds of plants eat animals."*
>
> ❝ *I wonder how the plants trap the animals."*
>
> ❝ *I wonder how the plant knows there is an animal on it."*

Have a few volunteers share their ideas with the class.

▶ USE "WORDS YOU KNOW" TO HELP STRUCTURE THE READ-ALOUD

Show pages 30–31, point to each picture, read the name of each plant, and write the names *bladderwort, pitcher plant, sundew plant,* and *Venus's-flytrap* where everyone can see them.

Tell the students that they will learn about each of these plants from today's read-aloud. Remind them to listen carefully to learn how each kind traps and eats animals. Explain that you will stop a few times during the read-aloud to give partners a chance to discuss what they learn.

Teacher Note

As in the previous lesson, the students will share with their partners only—not with the whole group—at all but the first read-aloud stopping point.

▶ READ ALOUD WITH BRIEF SECTION INTRODUCTIONS

Read *Plants that Eat Animals* aloud, showing the photographs, reading the accompanying captions, and stopping as described below. Before you read about each type of plant, point to its name on the list you wrote during Step 3.

Suggested Vocabulary

minerals: things in food that are needed by people, animals, and plants to stay strong and healthy (p. 3)

wetlands: land where there is a lot of water in the soil (p. 7)

boggy: wet and spongy (p. 12)

pitcher: container with an open top for holding and pouring liquid (p. 18)

Read page 3 aloud. Stop and ask:

Q *What do all plants need to grow? Where do most plants get what they need?*

Have one or two students respond to each question. Then reread page 3 and continue reading. At the end of page 5, tell the students that the next section you will read tells how a Venus's-flytrap gets its food. Read and stop after the caption:

[p. 11] "A Venus's-flytrap traps a cricket."

Teacher Note

Be ready to reread passages if necessary.

Ask:

Q *How does a Venus's-flytrap catch and eat insects?*

Have the students use "Turn to Your Partner" to discuss the question. Remind them to try to contribute ideas that are different from their partner's ideas.

Turn to Your Partner

After a minute, tell the students that the next part you will read tells about sundew plants. Resume reading and stop after:

[p. 17]   "The sundew is ready for another meal."

Have the students use "Turn to Your Partner" to discuss:

Q *How does a sundew catch and eat its food?*

After a minute, tell the students that the next part of the book tells about pitcher plants, another kind of insect-eating plant. Resume reading and stop after:

[p. 23]   "Flytrap pitcher plant"

Have the students use "Turn to Your Partner" to discuss:

Q *How do pitcher plants catch and kill their prey?*

After a minute, tell the students that the next section of the book tells about bladderwort plants. Resume reading and stop after:

[p. 27]   "…it opens up and sucks the animal inside."

Have the students use "Turn to Your Partner" to discuss:

Q *How do bladderworts catch their food?*

After a minute, resume reading and continue reading to the end of the book.

5▶ DISCUSS AS A WHOLE CLASS

Facilitate a whole-class discussion about what the students learned from the book. Use questions such as:

Q *What was the most interesting thing you learned about plants that eat animals?*

Q *What are you still wondering about plants that eat animals?*

> **Students might say:**
>
> ❝ *I wonder if a human can drink the liquid from a pitcher plant."*
>
> ❝ *I wonder whether the plants can eat any small animal."*
>
> ❝ *I wonder how the Venus's-flytrap closes up when an insect touches the hair."*

Explain that in the coming weeks the students will continue to read and listen to nonfiction books.

6▶ REFLECT ON WORKING TOGETHER

Turn to Your Partner • • • • •

Ask the students to tell their partner one helpful thing their partner did while they were discussing the book today. Then have a few volunteers share with the class how their partner was helpful.

Individualized Daily Reading

7▶ DOCUMENT IDR CONFERENCES/ WRITE IN THE "IDR JOURNAL"

Have the students read independently for up to 20 minutes.

Use the "IDR Conference Notes" record sheet to conduct and document individual conferences.

At the end of independent reading, have the students write about an interesting fact they learned from their reading in their "IDR Journal." Have them share their writing with their partner.

Day 3
Independent Strategy Practice

Materials

- Nonfiction books at appropriate levels for independent reading

- A small self-stick note for each student

- *Student Book* page 5

- *Assessment Record Book*

Lesson Purpose

Students:

▶ Discuss nonfiction books read independently.

▶ Identify and write about what they learn from their reading.

▶ Share their thinking with one another.

Teacher Note

Today the students will practice rereading. They will read a section of the text independently twice, once for surface understanding and again to identify something to share with their partner. You will ask the students to read for 5 minutes then stop and reread the section, paying close attention to what they learn.

1 REVIEW THE WEEK

Have partners sit together. Remind the students that in the past couple of weeks they heard nonfiction books and talked about what they learned from the books and what they wondered. Review that nonfiction books tell about real people, places, events, or things. Explain that today the students will think about what they learn as they read nonfiction books independently.

ELL Note

Note challenging vocabulary in the students' books and have brief discussions with individual students to define words as they read.

2 READ INDEPENDENTLY WITHOUT STOPPING

Have the students use a self-stick note to mark the place where they begin to read.

Have them read independently for 5 minutes.

3 REREAD INDEPENDENTLY AND IDENTIFY INFORMATION LEARNED

Stop the students after 5 minutes. Tell them that they will reread, starting again at the self-stick note, to find something interesting or surprising that they want to share with their partner.

Have the students return to their self-stick note and reread that section of the book for 5 minutes.

4 DISCUSS WHAT THE STUDENTS LEARNED IN PAIRS

Stop the students after 5 minutes. Have them share with their partner the title of their book and one thing that was interesting or surprising in it.

Class Comprehension Assessment

Circulate among the students and ask yourself:

Q *Are the students able to identify and describe something interesting or surprising they learned from their text?*

Record your observations on page 23 of the *Assessment Record Book*.

---

5 WRITE ABOUT WHAT THE STUDENTS LEARNED

Have the students turn to *Student Book* page 5, "What I Learned," and explain that you would like them to write one or two sentences in their own words about what they learned from their reading.

6 DISCUSS INDEPENDENT READING AS A CLASS

Have a few volunteers share something they learned. Remind them to say the title of their book before sharing. Ask questions such as:

Q *What new or interesting information did you learn from your book?*

Q *What are you wondering about what you have read?*

Share your observations of ways partners worked together, and explain that partners will continue to talk about what they are learning from their independent reading books and what they are wondering.

Overview *of* Week 4

...shes *(A True Book)*
...Melissa Stewart
...ildren's Press, 2001)

...nopsis
...is book describes the
...avior, physical
...its, and life cycles
...fish.

Alternative Books

- *It Could Still Be a Butterfly*
  by Allan Fowler

- *It Could Still Be a Flower*
  by Allan Fowler

Comprehension Focus

- Students *use schema* to help them understand a nonfiction text.

- Students identify what they learn from the text.

- Students *use wondering/questioning* to make sense of the text.

- Students informally *explore expository text features*.

Social Development Focus

- Students relate the value of responsibility to their behavior.

- Students develop the group skill of contributing ideas that are different from other people's ideas.

Materials

- *Fishes*
- Scratch paper and a pencil

Day 1
Read-Aloud

Lesson Purpose

Students:

▶ Identify what they learn from a nonfiction text.

▶ *Use wondering/questioning* to make sense of the text.

▶ Informally *explore expository text features.*

▶ Contribute ideas that are different from other people's ideas.

▶ REVIEW CONTRIBUTING DIFFERENT IDEAS

Have partners sit together. Remind the students that they have been working on contributing ideas that are different from other people's ideas during partner and class discussions. Tell them that the nonfiction book they will begin listening to today contains lots of new information. Point out that if everyone remembers a different idea during discussions, together the class can remember more facts from the book.

▶ INTRODUCE *FISHES* AND EXPLORE EXPOSITORY TEXT FEATURES

Show the cover of *Fishes* and read the title and author's name aloud. Explain that the photo on the cover shows a school of fish called "French grunts." Display the copyright page and explain that you learned what the photo shows by reading information on this page, which also tells which company published the book (Children's Press) and when it was published (in 2001).

Next, show the table of contents on page 3, and explain that a table of contents gives information about the topics in a book and pages where these topics can be found. Read a few of the chapter titles aloud.

Teacher Note

You may wish to explain that both *fish* and *fishes* can be used to mean more than one fish.

Ask:

Q *What do you think you will learn about fishes from this book?*

Have one or two students share their ideas; then explain that you will read the first chapter, "What Is a Fish?" As before, you will stop during the reading to give partners a chance to share what they are learning from the book.

▶ READ CHAPTER 1 OF *FISHES* ALOUD

Read Chapter 1 of *Fishes* aloud, showing the photographs, reading the accompanying captions, and stopping as described below.

Read the first sentence on page 5 aloud twice, and have the students use "Think, Pair, Share" to briefly discuss what they think of when they hear the word *fish*. Have a few volunteers share what they discussed with the class. Then read pages 4–5 aloud.

Tell the students that the next part of the chapter tells where fish live and how large or small they can be. Resume reading and stop after:

[p. 7] "…about the size of the eraser on a pencil."

Ask, and have the students use "Turn to Your Partner" to discuss:

Q *What did you find out about fishes in the part I just read?*

After a moment, tell the students that the next part you will read tells about fishes' bodies. Resume reading and stop after:

[p. 9] "The white area behind this hogfish's mouth is its gills."

Ask, and have the students use "Turn to Your Partner" to discuss:

Q *What did you learn about fishes' bodies?*

ELL Note

English language learners may benefit from previewing the book prior to the read-aloud.

Think, Pair, Share

Turn to Your Partner

4▶ DISCUSS WHAT THE STUDENTS LEARNED AND WONDER

Facilitate a whole-class discussion about what the students learned about fish. Remind the students to try to contribute different ideas from those their classmates mention. Use questions such as:

Q *What did you hear about fish that you already knew?*

Q *What new or surprising information about fish did you learn?*

Q *Now that you have learned some information about fish, what are you wondering about them?*

As the students share, jot down some of their questions on scratch paper, making particular note of those about fishes' bodies, since you will read about this topic on Day 2. Tell them that some of their questions may be answered in the next lesson, when they will hear a chapter of *Fishes* called "A Fish's Body."

Individualized Daily Reading

5▶ READ INDEPENDENTLY AND WONDER/ DOCUMENT IDR CONFERENCES

Remind the students that one of the strategies readers use is to wonder as they read. Explain that during today's independent reading you would like them to use self-stick notes to mark one or two places where the reading made them stop and wonder.

Have the students read nonfiction independently for up to 20 minutes.

Use the "IDR Conference Notes" record sheet to conduct and document individual conferences.

At the end of independent reading, have a few students share with the class.

> **Teacher Note**
>
> If necessary, model the procedure using a text you are reading.

Day 2
Strategy Lesson

Materials

- *Fishes*
- Your jotted questions from Day 1
- *Student Book* page 6
- *Student Book*, IDR Journal section

Lesson Purpose

Students:

▸ Identify what they learn from a nonfiction text.

▸ *Use wondering/questioning* to make sense of the text.

▸ Informally *explore expository text features.*

▸ Contribute ideas that are different from other people's ideas.

1 ▸ REVIEW THE PREVIOUS LESSON

Have partners sit together. Show the photo on page 9 of *Fishes* and remind the students that in the previous lesson they learned what a fish's gills and backbone are for. If necessary, reread page 8 to help the students recall what they learned about these body parts.

2 ▸ INTRODUCE CHAPTER 3, "A FISH'S BODY"

Show page 3, the "Contents" page. Point to and read the third chapter title, "A Fish's Body," aloud. Ask a volunteer what page it begins on (page 20). Tell the students that today you will skip ahead to this chapter so they can continue to learn about fishes' bodies.

Show pages 20–21 and read the chapter title aloud. Use the notes you jotted down on Day 1 to remind the students of any questions they had about fishes' bodies. Suggest that this chapter may answer some of their questions.

Explain that you will stop during the reading to give the students opportunities to talk about information they are learning.

ELL Note

English Language Learners may benefit from previewing the book prior to the read-aloud.

▶ READ ALOUD WITH BRIEF SECTION INTRODUCTIONS

Read pages 20–29 of *Fishes* aloud, stopping as described below.

Suggested Vocabulary

slim: thin (p. 23)

narrow: not wide; thin (p. 23)

cruise: travel smoothly and easily (p. 23)

broad: wide (p. 23)

shingles: flat pieces of wood that are put in overlapping rows to cover roofs and outside walls (p. 23)

suit of armor: metal suit of clothes used as protection in battle (p.24)

grasp: hold (p. 25)

nostrils: openings used for breathing and smelling (p. 26)

algae: small plants without roots or stems that grow under water (p. 27)

coral: colonies of tiny sea creatures (p. 27)

mussels: sea creatures that have a two-part, usually black, shell (p. 28)

Tell the students that the first part of the chapter tells about fishes' fins. Read pages 20–21 aloud and stop to point out the labeled photograph on page 21. Read the labels aloud and have two or three volunteers tell how a fish uses each kind of fin. Then reread pages 20–21 and continue reading. Stop after:

> [p. 23] "…but they are better at turning quickly."

Turn to Your Partner

Have the students use "Turn to Your Partner" to discuss:

Q *What did you learn about fishes' fins?*

After a moment, tell the students that the next part you will read tells about fishes' scales. Resume reading and stop after:

> [p. 25] "You can tell a fish's age by counting the number of growth rings on its scales."

Have the students use "Turn to Your Partner" to discuss:

Q *What did you learn about fishes' scales?*

After a minute, point out that fish have some body parts—such as fins, tails, and scales—that people don't have. However, they have other parts—such as eyes—that people have, too. Tell the students that the next part you will read tells about fishes' eyes, mouths, and teeth.

Skip the last paragraph on page 25 and the first one on page 26, and resume reading with the second paragraph on page 26. Continue reading and stop after:

> [p. 28] "Fishes with sharp, pointed teeth hunt other fishes."

Have the students use "Turn to Your Partner" to discuss:

Q *What did you learn about fishes' eyes, mouths, and teeth?*

After a minute, tell the students that the last part of the chapter tells what different-sized fish eat. Resume reading and stop after:

> [p. 29] "A large koi carp is about to swallow a small goldfish."

Have the students use "Turn to Your Partner" to discuss:

Q *What do small, medium-sized, and large fishes eat?*

▶ 4 DISCUSS AND WRITE ABOUT WHAT THE STUDENTS LEARNED AND WONDER

Facilitate a brief whole-class discussion of the chapter. Use the photos, labels, and captions to review the facts in it. Ask:

Q *What was the most interesting or surprising thing you learned from this chapter?*

Use the notes you jotted down on Day 1 to briefly review what the students wondered about fish. Ask:

Q *What are you still wondering about fish?*

Teacher Note

If necessary, model writing sample sentences on the board. (For example: "I learned that big fish eat smaller fish." or "I wonder if sharks ever try to eat fish that are bigger than they are.")

Have the students turn to *Student Book* page 6, "Fishes." Explain that they will write one thing they learned and one thing they wondered about as they listened to the book.

5 SHARE WRITING AS A CLASS

Have volunteers read to the class the sentences they wrote in their *Student Book*. Be ready to reread parts of the text or show photos that support what the students wrote.

Tell the students that you will not read the rest of *Fishes* aloud, but that it will be available for independent reading.

Individualized Daily Reading

6 WRITE IN THE "IDR JOURNAL"/ DOCUMENT IDR CONFERENCES

Explain that during today's independent reading you would like the students to use self-stick notes to mark one or two places where they stop to wonder while they are reading. Explain that later they will write about what they learned and what they wonder in their "IDR Journal."

Have the students read nonfiction independently for up to 20 minutes.

Use the "IDR Conference Notes" record sheet to conduct and document individual conferences.

At the end of independent reading, have the students write about what they learned from today's reading and what they wonder in their "IDR Journal."

Extensions

▷ **LEARN MORE ABOUT FISH**

Use the additional resources listed on pages 44–45 in *Fishes* to have the students find out more about fish. As a class, discuss answers to the students' questions and other interesting information they learn during their search.

▷ **EXPLORE AN INDEX**

Display page 47 of the book and explain that this page, the index, tells where to look in *Fishes* for information on topics like feelers, moray eels, and seahorses. Point out that the topics are listed in alphabetical order. Read aloud some of the items listed and invite volunteers to pick one or two for the class to look up and read together.

Materials

- Nonfiction books at appropriate levels for independent reading

- A small self-stick note for each student

- *Student Book* page 7

- *Assessment Record Book*

Day 3
Independent Strategy Practice

Lesson Purpose

Students:

▶ Read nonfiction books independently.

▶ Identify what they learn from a nonfiction text.

▶ Share their thinking.

▶ REVIEW THE WEEK

Have partners sit together. Remind the students that they have been listening to nonfiction books and talking to their partner about what they learned and wondered as they listened.

Explain that today the students will continue to think about what they learn and wonder as they read independently. Explain that they will read a section of their book twice.

▶ READ INDEPENDENTLY WITHOUT STOPPING

Have the students use a self-stick note to mark the place where they begin to read. Have them read independently for 5 minutes.

▶ REREAD INDEPENDENTLY AND IDENTIFY WHAT THE STUDENTS LEARNED AND WONDER

Stop the students after 5 minutes. Tell them that they will reread, starting again at the self-stick note. Ask them to find an interesting piece of information to share with their partner. Encourage them to also pay attention to "I wonder…" statements or questions that come to mind as they read.

Have the students reread for 5 minutes.

Teacher Note

Note challenging vocabulary in the students' independent reading books and have brief discussions with individual students to define words as they read independently.

Teacher Note

Circulate as the students work. Notice whether they are able to identify questions that come to mind based on what they learn from their reading. Ask individual students:

Q *What are you wondering about [popcorn]?*

Q *What part of your book made you wonder about that?*

---

4 ▶ DISCUSS WHAT THE STUDENTS LEARNED AND WONDER IN PAIRS

Stop the students after 5 minutes. Have them share with their partner the title of their book, something they learned from their reading, and something they wonder about their book's topic.

Turn to Your Partner

5 ▶ WRITE ABOUT WHAT THEY LEARNED AND WONDER

Have the students turn to *Student Book* page 7, "What I Learned and Wonder" and explain that you would like them to write one or two sentences in their own words about what they learned and wonder from their reading.

Class Comprehension Assessment

Circulate among the students as they work. Ask yourself:

Q *Are the students able to identify and describe what they have learned?*

Q *Do they wonder about things that are connected to their texts?*

Record your observations on page 24 of the *Assessment Record Book*.

---

6 ▶ DISCUSS INDEPENDENT READING AS A CLASS

Have a few volunteers share something they learned and something they wonder about their book's topic. Remind them to say the title of their book before sharing. Ask questions such as:

Q *What new or interesting information did you learn from your book?*

Q *What are you wondering about what you have read?*

Teacher Note

If you want to give the students more experience thinking about what they learned and wonder in independent reading, repeat this lesson using an alternative book and *Student Book* page 8.

▷ REFLECT ON WORKING TOGETHER

Facilitate a brief discussion about how the students took responsibility for themselves. Ask:

Q *How did you act in a responsible way during independent reading time? Why is that important?*

Overview *of* Week 5

POP! A Book About Bubbles
by Kimberly Brubaker Bradley, photographs by Margaret Miller (HarperCollins, 2001)

Synopsis
The book explains how bubbles are made, why they are always round, and why they pop.

Alternative Books

• *What Makes a Shadow?*
  by Clyde Robert Bulla

• *Dogs and Puppies*
  by J. I. Anderson

Comprehension Focus

• Students identify what they learn from a nonfiction text.

• Students *use schema and wondering/questioning* to make sense of the text.

Social Development Focus

• Students relate the value of responsibility to their behavior.

• Students develop the group skill of contributing ideas that are different from other people's ideas.

▶ **Do Ahead**

• Prepare to model wondering in independent reading (see Day 3, Step 2 on page 270).

Materials

- *POP! A Book About Bubbles*

Day 1
Read-Aloud/Strategy Lesson

Lesson Purpose

Students:

▶ Identify what they learn from a nonfiction text.

▶ *Wonder* about the text.

▶ Contribute ideas that are different from other people's ideas.

1 ▶ GET READY TO WORK TOGETHER

Have partners sit together. Explain that again this week the students will listen to a nonfiction book and share different ideas with their partner. Remind the students that readers sometimes make connections and wonder as they read to better understand a book. Explain that the students will use these strategies as they listen to today's read-aloud.

2 ▶ INTRODUCE *POP!*

Show the cover of *POP! A Book About Bubbles* and read the title and names of the author and photographer aloud. Ask:

Q *Have you ever blown bubbles? Tell us about it.*

Have a few students share their experiences with the class.

▶ **READ THE FIRST HALF OF *POP!* ALOUD**

Tell the students that the first part of the book tells what bubbles are and how you can make them. Read pages 5–15 of *POP! A Book About Bubbles* aloud, showing the photographs, and stopping as described below.

Suggested Vocabulary

wand: a thin stick or rod (p. 5; refer to the photograph)
solution: a mixture made up of something dissolved in liquid (p. 5)
shimmers: shines (p. 6)
corn syrup: sweet, sticky liquid (p. 10)

Stop after:

[p. 9]   "All bubbles are round."

Ask:

Q   *Based on what you heard, what are you wondering about bubbles?*

Have a couple of students share their thinking with the class.

Reread the last sentence on page 9 and continue reading to the bottom of page 10. Stop and tell the students you will reread page 10, and ask them to listen carefully for how bubbles are made. Reread page 10 and ask:

Q   *What did you learn about how bubbles are made?*

Have one or two students share their thinking with the class.

Reread the last sentence on page 10 and continue reading to the end of page 15.

ELL Note

English Language Learners may benefit from previewing pages 5–15 and hearing the suggested vocabulary briefly defined prior to the read-aloud.

4 DISCUSS THE READING AS A CLASS

Ask:

> **Q** *We talked at the beginning about blowing bubbles. Does anything in the book remind you of experiences you have had or things you have noticed while blowing bubbles?*

Turn to Your Partner • • • •

Have the students use "Turn to Your Partner" to discuss the question; then have a few students share their ideas with the class.

Explain that you will read the second half of the book tomorrow.

Individualized Daily Reading

5 REVIEW THE "READING COMPREHENSION STRATEGIES" CHART

Refer to the "Reading Comprehension Strategies" chart and review the strategies on it. Encourage the students to use these strategies to make sense of their reading.

Have the students read nonfiction books independently for up to 20 minutes.

As the students read, circulate among them and talk to individuals about their reading. Ask questions such as:

> **Q** *What is your book about? What's happening in your book right now?*

> **Q** *Are you wondering about anything so far? If so, what?*

> **Q** *What strategies are you using to help you understand the reading?*

At the end of independent reading, have the students share what they read as a whole class. Ask questions such as:

Q *What is a reading comprehension strategy on the chart you used when reading today? Where did you use it? How did it help you understand the story?*

Extension

▶ MAKE AND OBSERVE BUBBLES

Use the instructions on page 32 of *POP!* to have the students make and observe bubbles. You may want to begin by having pairs read page 32 together, and then as a class discuss the ingredients needed and the steps for making the bubble solution. After the students have made and observed their bubbles, discuss their observations and relate them to the information in the book.

Materials

- *POP! A Book About Bubbles*
- *Student Book,* IDR Journal section

Day 2
Read-Aloud/Strategy Lesson

Lesson Purpose

Students:

▶ Identify what they learn from a nonfiction text.

▶ *Wonder* about the text.

▶ Contribute ideas that are different from other people's ideas.

▶ REVIEW THE FIRST HALF OF *POP!*

Remind the students that in the last lesson they used wondering and making connections to learn about bubbles in the book *POP!* Tell them that today they will use visualizing to help them remember the first half of the book.

Ask the students to close their eyes and think about blowing bubbles as you read pages from the first half of the book. Read pages 6 and 9 to the students while they have their eyes closed. Briefly discuss:

Q *What did you see in your mind?*

Tell the students that you will read the second half of the book today, and that you would like them to think about new things they learn about bubbles.

ELL Note

English Language Learners may benefit from previewing pages 16–31 and hearing the suggested vocabulary words briefly defined prior to the read-aloud.

▶ READ THE SECOND HALF OF *POP!*

Read pages 16–30, stopping as described on the next page.

Suggested Vocabulary

evenly: equally, the same amount (p. 19)

shrink: become smaller (p. 20)

stream: a steady flow (p. 29)

Stop at the end of page 20. Tell the students that you will reread the section, and ask them to listen for new things they learn about bubbles. Reread pages 16–20. Ask:

Q *What new things did you learn about bubbles from these pages?*

Have one or two students share their thinking with the class. Reread the last two sentences on page 20 and continue reading to the next stop:

[p. 23] "…higher and higher, then pop!"

Q *What are you wondering right now about bubbles in soda?*

Have one or two students share their thinking with the class. Reread the sentence on page 23 and continue reading to the next stop:

[p. 24] "Water and juice aren't sticky like soap solution, so the bubbles pop right away."

Q *What are you wondering right now?*

Have one or two students share their thinking with the class. Reread the last sentence on page 24 and continue reading to the next stop:

[p. 26] "Wherever they aren't touching the glass or each other, they will be round."

Have one or two students share their thinking with the class. Reread the last sentence on page 26 and continue reading to the end of the page 30.

Turn to Your Partner • • • • •

3 DISCUSS *POP!* IN PAIRS AND AS A CLASS

First in pairs, then as a class, discuss the following questions. Remind the students to try to contribute ideas that are different from other people's ideas. Ask:

Q   *What new things did you learn about bubbles in today's reading?*

Q   *What are you still wondering about bubbles?*

Q   *What are some things that you would like to try with bubbles after hearing this book?*

4 REFLECT ON CONTRIBUTING DIFFERENT IDEAS

Briefly discuss how the students did contributing ideas that were different from other people's ideas. Ask:

Q   *Give us an example of a time in today's lesson when someone else said what you were going to say, and you thought of a different idea to say.*

Q   *Was it hard or easy to think of something different to say?*

Encourage the students to continue to use this skill during class discussions throughout the day. Explain that they will have an opportunity to think about what they are learning and to wonder in their independent reading tomorrow.

Individualized Daily Reading

5 DOCUMENT IDR CONFERENCES/ WRITE IN THE "IDR JOURNAL"

Explain that during today's independent reading you would like the students to use self-stick notes to mark one or two places where they stop and wonder about what they are reading. Explain that they will write about what they learned and what they wonder in their "IDR Journal."

Have the students read independently for up to 20 minutes.

Use the "IDR Conference Notes" record sheet to conduct and document individual conferences.

At the end of independent reading, have the students write about what they learned and what they wonder in their "IDR Journal."

Extension

▷ **BUBBLE EXPERIMENTS**

Use the instructions on page 33 of *POP!* and experiment with bubbles to answer the questions: "Are bubbles always round?" and "How slow can you blow?" Have the students predict answers and work in pairs to confirm or reject their predictions. As a class, discuss the outcomes of the experiments.

Materials

- Nonfiction text for teacher modeling

- A variety of nonfiction books at appropriate levels for independent reading.

- *Student Book* page 9

- "Reading Comprehension Strategies" chart

- *Assessment Record Book*

Day 3
Independent Strategy Practice

Lesson Purpose

Students:

▶ Read nonfiction texts independently.

▶ *Wonder* about the texts.

▶ Identify what they learn from the texts.

▶ Share their thinking.

▶ REVIEW THE WEEK

Have partners sit together. Remind the students that this week they listened to *POP! A Book About Bubbles* and talked about questions they had about bubbles. They also shared their thinking with one another and tried to contribute ideas that were different from other people's ideas. Tell the students that at the end of the lesson they will talk about how they worked with their partner throughout this unit.

▶ MODEL WONDERING
BEFORE READING NONFICTION TEXT

Explain that before they begin to read today partners will talk about what they wonder about the topic of their independent reading book.

Model wondering before reading by briefly introducing the nonfiction text you selected. Examine the cover of the book and look at several pages, commenting on photographs or illustrations. Then read the first two or three sentences in the book and wonder aloud.

Model writing several "I wonder" statements where everyone can see them.

Teacher Note

Have the questions you will ask in mind ahead of time so this modeling goes smoothly.

3▶ WONDER BEFORE READING INDEPENDENTLY

Have the students look at the front and back covers and the photographs or illustrations in their book and wonder quietly to themselves about its topic. After a few moments, have the students share what they are wondering with their partner.

• • • • • • **Turn to Your Partner**

4▶ WRITE "WHAT I WONDER BEFORE READING" STATEMENTS

Have the students turn to *Student Book* page 9, "What I Wonder Before Reading." Tell them that they will write one or two "I wonder" statements about the topic of their book in their *Student Book*. Refer to the statements you modeled writing and briefly review them.

Have the students write their statements in their *Student Book*.

Class Comprehension Assessment

Circulate among the students as they work. Ask yourself:

Q *Are the students able to wonder about a topic prior to reading?*

Q *Is their wondering connected to what they are previewing?*

Record your observations on page 25 of the *Assessment Record Book*.

5▶ READ INDEPENDENTLY

Have the students read independently for 10–15 minutes.

6▶ DISCUSS INDEPENDENT READING AS A CLASS

First in pairs, then as a class, discuss questions such as:

• • • • • • **Turn to Your Partner**

Q *What did you wonder about before you began reading?*

Teacher Note

This is the last week of Unit 6. You will reassign partners for Unit 7.

Q *Were your questions answered in the book? If so, explain.*

Q *What other questions do you have now that you've read some of the book?*

Tell the students that looking over a book before reading helps them get ready to listen and understand.

▷ **REFLECT ON WORKING TOGETHER**

Facilitate a brief discussion about how the students worked with their partner during the past five weeks. Ask questions such as:

Q *How did contributing different ideas from your partner help you think about the reading?*

Q *What were some ways you acted responsibly during reading time?*

Q *What will you do [the same way/differently] the next time you work with a partner?*

Give the students time to thank their partner.

Individual Comprehension Assessment

Before continuing with Unit 7, take this opportunity to assess individual students' progress in thinking about what they are learning and using *wondering/questioning* to help them understand nonfiction text. Please refer to pages 38–39 in the *Assessment Record Book* for instructions.

IDR Conference Week

Take a break from the lessons in the upcoming week, and use your daily reading block for IDR. As the students read books at their level independently, you will have an opportunity to confer with every student and document these conferences using the "IDR Conference Notes" record sheet. Over the year each student's accumulated IDR conference notes will become a record of his progress over time.

Continue with Unit 7, Week 1 in the following week.

Unit 7 ▶ Exploring Important Ideas

Unit 7 ▶ Exploring Important Ideas

During this unit, the students explore important ideas in texts and use inference informally to think about what is important in text. Socially, they relate the value of fairness to their partner work as they develop the group skill of sharing their partner time. They reflect on this sharing in a class meeting. They also practice giving reasons to support their thinking.

Week 1 ▶ **"Wild Rides"**
by Lev Grossman
from *TIME For Kids* [May 10, 2002]

"Summer of the Shark"
from *TIME For Kids*
[September 14, 2001]

"A Nose for the Arts"
from *TIME For Kids*
[December 14, 2001]

Week 2 ▶ *Me First*
by Helen Lester

Week 3 ▶ *Big Al*
by Andrew Clements

Overview
of Week 1

"Wild Rides" by Lev Grossman from
TIME For Kids [May 10, 2002]

www.timeforkids.com

"Summer of the Shark" from *TIME For Kids*
[September 14, 2001]

www.timeforkids.com

"A Nose for the Arts" from *TIME For Kids*
[December 14, 2001]

www.timeforkids.com

Alternative Resources
···

- *TIME For Kids* Magazine
  www.timeforkids.com

- kids.discovery.com

Comprehension Focus

- Students *explore important ideas* in texts.

- Students *use inference* informally to think about what is important in text.

Social Development Focus

- Students relate the value of fairness to their partner work.

- Students develop the group skills of giving reasons to support their thinking and sharing their partner time in a fair way.

▶ Do Ahead

- Collect a variety of newspapers, articles, and magazines at various reading levels for the students to read during IDR. (See "About Important Ideas" on page 278.)

Materials

- "Wild Rides"
  (see pages 284–285)

Teacher Note

Provide a variety of newspapers and magazines for independent reading.

Day 1
Read-Aloud/Strategy Lesson

Lesson Purpose

Students:

▶ Begin working with a new partner.

▶ Hear and discuss an article.

▶ Explore important ideas in an article.

About Important Ideas

The focus in this unit is on *determining important ideas*, a powerful strategy for helping readers understand and retain what they read. In the *Making Meaning* program, the focus is on helping the students explore the important ideas in a story or article, rather than identify a single "main idea." The students explore the important ideas and support their opinions with evidence from the text. At times, the students have to infer to determine the important ideas.

In Week 1, the students hear magazine articles read aloud. In Weeks 2 and 3, the students explore important ideas in narrative text.

▶ PAIR STUDENTS AND GET READY TO WORK TOGETHER

Assign partners and have them sit together. Review that over the past weeks the students have practiced several social skills— taking turns talking and listening, giving reasons for their thinking, and contributing ideas that are different from other people's ideas. Explain that in the next few weeks, they will continue to focus on giving reasons for their thinking and sharing their partner time in a fair way.

Ask:

Q *What are some things you can do today to make sure your new partner feels comfortable sharing?*

Have a few students share their thinking.

Explain that *thinking about what is important* is a strategy that readers use to make sense of text. Explain that when authors write articles and stories, there are things they really want people to learn and remember. Those are the important ideas.

Tell the students that in this unit, they will hear magazine articles and stories and use the comprehension strategies they know to explore the important ideas in what they hear and read.

2▸ REVIEW NONFICTION AND INTRODUCE ARTICLES

Review that in the last few weeks, the students heard nonfiction books and stories about people, plants, and animals. They talked about what they learned and what they wondered. Explain that today they will listen to an article from a magazine called *TIME For Kids,* and they will think about the topic of the article and the important information in it. Point out that magazine and newspaper articles are another kind of nonfiction. Articles give information or the writer's opinion about a particular topic. (You may want to show examples of magazines, such as *Ranger Rick, TIME For Kids, Scholastic News,* and *Weekly Reader.*)

3▸ INTRODUCE "WILD RIDES"

Read the title of the article "Wild Rides" and the date of the article. Ask:

Q *What do you think the article "Wild Rides" might be about?*

> **Students might say:**
>
> ❝ *I think it might be about riding wild horses."*
>
> ❝ *It might be about taking a wild ride on a skateboard, because some people go over bumps on a skateboard."*
>
> ❝ *It could be a car race because racers drive very fast."*

Explain that you will read the article twice. During the first reading, the students will discuss what the article is about. During the second reading, they will talk about what they think is important in it.

▶ READ "WILD RIDES" ALOUD

Read "Wild Rides" aloud, slowly and clearly, stopping as described below.

> **Suggested Vocabulary**
>
> **engineers:** people who design and build machines, cars, bridges, roads, or other structures
>
> **model:** small or miniature version of the real thing
>
> **verdict:** a decision or opinion

Read and stop after:

> "This year's new rides are the wildest ever!"

Ask:

Q *What does the title "Wild Rides" mean?*

Have two or three students share their thinking with the class. Then read the heading "Picking Up Speed" and read the next paragraph. Stop after:

> "How did they get that fast? Computers."

Ask:

Q *What are some things you have learned so far about roller coasters?*

Have two or three students share their thinking with the class. Reread the last sentence before the stop and continue reading through the next paragraph. Stop after:

> "'There are limits that you don't go over, because you can break a bone,' says Schilke. Yikes!"

Ask:

Q *What else did you learn about roller coasters in the part I just read?*

Have the students use "Turn to Your Partner" to discuss what they have learned. Then have two or three students share their thinking with the class. Reread the last sentence before the stop and continue reading to the end of the article.

Turn to Your Partner

▶ 5 REREAD THE ARTICLE AND DISCUSS IMPORTANT IDEAS

Ask:

Q *If someone asked you what this article is about, what would you tell them?*

Have two or three students share their thinking with the class. Explain that you will reread the article, and the students will discuss what is important to know in different parts of the article.

Read and stop again after:

> "This year's new rides are the wildest ever!"

Ask:

Q *What is the most important thing to remember from the part you just heard?*

> **Teacher Note**
> If the students have difficulty identifying the important ideas, you may need to model the strategy.

Have the students use "Think, Pair, Share" to discuss the question. Then have two or three students share their thinking with the class.

Think, Pair, Share

Read the section heading "Picking Up Speed," and continue through the next two paragraphs. Stop again after:

> "'There are limits that you don't go over, because you can break a bone,' says Schilke. Yikes!"

Ask:

Q *Why are computers important for building roller coasters?*

Think, Pair, Share ● ● ● ● ●

Have the students use "Think, Pair, Share" to discuss the question. Then have two or three students share their thinking with the class.

Read the last sentence before the stop and continue reading to the end of the article.

6 DISCUSS THINKING ABOUT IMPORTANT IDEAS

Review that in today's lesson, the students listened to an article and thought about what they learned and what was important. Explain that when authors write articles and stories, there are things they really want people to learn and remember. Those are the important ideas.

7 REFLECT ON WORKING TOGETHER

Facilitate a brief discussion about how the students did making their new partners feel comfortable sharing.

Individualized Daily Reading

8 READ INDEPENDENTLY/DOCUMENT IDR CONFERENCES

Have the students read nonfiction (books or articles) independently for up to 20 minutes.

Use the "IDR Conference Notes" record sheet to conduct and document individual conferences. Continue to encourage the students to self-monitor as they read independently.

At the end of independent reading, have the students share their reading with their partner. As the students share, circulate and listen, observe the students' behaviors and responses, and make notes.

Extension

▷ READ TITLES AND ARTICLES

Collect a variety of articles at various reading levels. Have partners sit together, and distribute an article to each pair. Have partners read the title, predict what the article might be about, read the article, and discuss it. Have each pair share their title and article with another pair, small group, or the class.

Article

from **timeforkids.com**

News Scoop Edition (May 10, 2002)

Wild Rides by Lev Grossman

If you've ever been on a roller coaster, you know what it's like: You go up, you go down (boy do you go down!), maybe you go upside down. Then before you know it, it's over. But as ride designers learn new tricks, coasters are getting faster, bigger, and wilder. This year's new rides are the wildest ever!

Picking Up Speed

The first true roller coaster in America was built at Coney Island in New York City in 1884. It rolled along at 6 miles per hour. Now, coasters can reach speeds of 100 miles per hour! How did they get that fast? Computers.

Before engineers build a new roller coaster, they make a computer model that shows how it will run. This helps them make it as safe—and scary—as possible. Allan Schilke is one of the best-known ride designers in the world. He created the ride called X. Computers help him figure out how fast the riders can safely go. "There are limits that you don't go over, because you can break a bone," says Schilke. Yikes!

Most riders have no clue about how coasters are created. They're just along for the ride. Joey Stilphen, 13, of Bay Village, Ohio, tried out the Wicked Twister at Cedar Point last week. His verdict: "It's awesome!"

Materials

* "Summer of the Shark"
  (see page 290)

Day 2
Read-Aloud/Strategy Lesson

Lesson Purpose

Students:

▶ *Explore important ideas* in an article.

▶ Give reasons to support their thinking.

▶ Share their partner time in a fair way.

1▶ GET READY TO WORK TOGETHER

Have partners sit together. Remind the students that in the last lesson they listened to a magazine article and talked about the important ideas in it. Explain that today you will read another magazine article aloud, and they will discuss the important ideas with their partner and the class. Explain that at the end of the lesson you will ask them to report how they did using their partner time fairly.

2▶ INTRODUCE "SUMMER OF THE SHARK"

Explain that today you will read another *TIME For Kids* article, called "Summer of the Shark." Ask:

Q *What do you think this article might be about?*

Have two or three students share their thinking with the class.

Explain that you will read the article twice. During the first reading, the students will discuss what they are learning. During the second reading, they will talk about the important ideas in the article.

▶ READ "SUMMER OF THE SHARK" ALOUD

Before reading the article, define the vocabulary word *odds*, and give an example. (For example, "The odds or chances of your meeting an elephant on your way home are very small. The odds of your meeting someone you know on your way home are much greater.")

Suggested Vocabulary

worldwide: around the world

odds: chances or likelihood of something happening

slim: small

ELL Vocabulary

English Language Learners may benefit from discussing additional vocabulary, including:

shark: a large and often fierce fish that feeds on meat and has very sharp teeth

seal: a sea mammal that lives in the coastal waters and has thick fur and flippers

shark attacks: sharks' attempts to bite people

splash: throw water around

lightning: a flash of light in the sky, usually during a storm

Read the first paragraph aloud twice. Continue reading and stop after:

> "That's when sharks hunt."

Ask:

Q *What have you learned about sharks so far?*

Have the students use "Turn to Your Partner" to discuss what they have learned.

Without sharing as a class, reread the last sentence and continue reading to the end of the article.

Have the students use "Turn to Your Partner" to discuss what they have learned. Have two or three students share their thinking with the class. Be ready to reread sentences to help the students recall what they heard.

ELL Note

If possible, show the students pictures of sharks and seals to enhance their understanding.

Teacher Note

If the students have difficulty discussing what they have learned in pairs, you may want to have a few students share with the class.

Teacher Note

If the students have difficulty identifying important ideas in the article, reread a section and model thinking aloud about the important idea. You might reread the first paragraph and say, "I think the really important idea in this part is that sharks don't really like to bite people. It says they prefer to eat seals."

Think, Pair, Share ● ● ● ● ●

4 ▶ REREAD AND DISCUSS IMPORTANT IDEAS

Explain that you will reread "Summer of the Shark." Then they will discuss the important ideas in the article.

Reread "Summer of the Shark" aloud, slowly and clearly. Facilitate a whole-class discussion of the article, using the following questions. Remind the students to give reasons for their thinking.

Q *What is this article about?*

Q *What are the important ideas about sharks in this article? Why do you think so?*

Have the students use "Think, Pair, Share" to discuss the questions before talking as a class.

> **Students might say:**
>
> ❝ *I think one important idea is that sharks really don't like to bite people. They only do it by mistake. The story says they might think a foot is a fish."*
>
> ❝ *I think another important idea is that people get in the way of sharks when sharks are hunting for food and confuse them. I think that because the article says people splash around in the ocean when sharks hunt."*
>
> ❝ *Sharks hunt in the morning and in the early evening. If you are a skin diver, this is important to know so you don't go diving at those times."*

Explain that in the next lesson partners will work together to read and discuss another article.

5 ▶ REFLECT ON WORKING TOGETHER

Facilitate a brief discussion about how the students did giving reasons to support their thinking and sharing their partner time fairly.

Explain that in the next lesson you will read another article, entitled "A Nose for the Arts."

Individualized Daily Reading

▷ READ INDEPENDENTLY/DOCUMENT IDR CONFERENCES

Have the students read nonfiction independently for up to 20 minutes.

Use the "IDR Conference Notes" record sheet to conduct and document individual conferences. Continue to encourage the students to self-monitor as they read independently.

At the end of independent reading, have the students discuss their reading with the class. Facilitate the discussion with questions such as:

Q *What do you like about what you read?*

Q *What have you learned so far? What information is really important?*

News Scoop Edition (September 14, 2001)

Summer of the Shark

Sharks don't really like to bite people. A great white shark prefers to eat a seal. A bull shark loves fish and even another shark! Then why was this summer full of scary news about shark attacks? Scientists say that is one good question.

Last year sharks bit 84 people worldwide. This year there have been 52 attacks so far. Most were in Florida.

One reason for the high numbers is that more people are in the ocean than ever before. Many splash around in the morning and early evening. That's when sharks hunt.

Sharks that attack humans are probably confused. They might mistake a human foot for a fish. "Sharks are not out to get humans," says scientist Dr. Robert Lea. "It is just humans sharing a spot in the ocean with sharks at the wrong time."

Don't panic. The odds of being attacked by a shark are slim. You are 30 times more likely to be hit by lightning!

Day 3
Read-Aloud/Strategy Lesson

Materials

· "A Nose for the Arts"
  (see pages 296–297)

· *Assessment Record Book*

· *Student Book,* IDR Journal
  section

Lesson Purpose

Students:

▶ *Identify important ideas* in an article.

▶ Give reasons to support their thinking.

▶ REVIEW THE WEEK

Have partners sit together. Review that in the previous lesson the
students listened to an article about sharks and explored the
important ideas in it. Explain that today, they will hear another
article and practice thinking about what they are learning and
what is important.

▶ INTRODUCE "A NOSE FOR THE ARTS"

Explain that today you will read another *TIME For Kids* article,
called "A Nose for the Arts." Make sure the students understand
the words *arts* and *artist*. Tell the students that the article is about
two artists named Boon Yang and Bird.

Explain that you will read the article twice. During the first
reading, the students will discuss what they are learning. During
the second reading, they will talk about the important ideas in
the article.

▶ READ "A NOSE FOR THE ARTS" ALOUD

Read "A Nose for the Arts" aloud, stopping as described on the
next page.

Suggested Vocabulary

streaks: long, thin marks or stripes

brush: make strokes or marks with a paintbrush

canvas: a surface for painting made from a strong cloth stretched over a wooden frame

orchestra: a large group of musicians who play their instruments together

conservation center: a place where an animal or a natural environment is protected

ELL Vocabulary
English Language Learners may benefit from discussing additional vocabulary, including:

elephant: (show a picture)

trunk: the long nose of an elephant, used for drinking, carrying and holding things, and feeding itself (refer to a picture)

museums: places where interesting objects of art, history, or science are displayed

CD: short for compact disc, a disc that stores music that can be played on a compact disc player

Read the first paragraph aloud. Stop after:

> "Bird and Boon Yang hold a paintbrush with a trunk!"

Ask:

Q *What is surprising about the artists Boon Yang and Bird?*

Have two or three students share their thinking with the class. Reread the last sentence before the stop and read the next two paragraphs. Stop after:

> "The money raised by selling CDs and paintings goes to an elephant-conservation center in Thailand."

Ask:

Q *What have you learned so far in this article?*

Teacher Note
If the students haven't realized that Boon Yang and Bird are elephants, reread the paragraph and ask them to listen carefully for information about the artists.

Turn to Your Partner • • • • •

Have the students use "Turn to Your Partner" to discuss what they have learned. Without sharing as a class, read the subtitle "Can Art Save Elephants?" and continue reading to the end of the article.

Ask:

Q *What did you learn in the last part you heard?*

Have the students use "Turn to Your Partner" to discuss what they have learned. Have two or three students share their thinking with the class.

▶ REREAD AND DISCUSS IMPORTANT IDEAS

Tell the students that you will reread the article, and this time, you would like them to think about what the important ideas in the article are. Before rereading, ask:

Q *If a friend asked you what "A Nose for the Arts" is about, what would you tell her?*

Have two or three students share their thinking with the class. Begin rereading and continue through the third paragraph. Stop after:

> "The money raised by selling CDs and paintings goes to an elephant-conservation center in Thailand."

Ask:

Q *What are one or two things the author really wants you to remember from this part?*

Have the students use "Think, Pair, Share" to discuss the question. •••••• **Think, Pair, Share**
Have two or three students share their thinking with the class. Read the subtitle "Can Art Save Elephants?" and continue reading to the end of the article. Ask:

Q *What do you think is really important to remember from the part I just read?*

Have the students use "Think, Pair, Share" to discuss what they have learned.

Class Comprehension Assessment

Circulate as partners share and ask yourself:

Q *Are the students able to identify what is important to remember or know?*

Record your observations on page 26 of the *Assessment Record Book*.

▷ REFLECT ON WORKING TOGETHER

Facilitate a brief discussion about how partners worked together. Ask:

Q *How did you do today sharing your partner time in a fair way?*

Explain that next week the students will have a chance to talk with their partner and with the class about the important ideas in a fiction story.

Individualized Daily Reading

▷ WRITE ABOUT AN IMPORTANT IDEA IN NONFICTION TEXT IN THE "IDR JOURNAL"

Tell the students that today they will write about an important idea in their reading in their "IDR Journal."

Have the students read nonfiction independently for up to 20 minutes.

As the students read, circulate among them. Observe their reading behavior and engagement with the text. Ask individual students questions such as:

Q   *What is your reading about?*

Q   *What are you learning?*

Q   *What is an important idea in this [article/book]?*

At the end of independent reading, have the students write about an important idea from today's reading in their "IDR Journal."

Extension

▷ THINK ABOUT THE TITLES AUTHORS CHOOSE

Point out that sometimes authors use clever titles like "A Nose for the Arts" to attract people's attention and make them curious about an article. At other times, they use titles that tell exactly what the article will be about, like "Summer of the Shark." Ask:

Q   *Do you think "A Nose for the Arts" is a good title for the article you heard today? Why or why not?*

Q   *What do you think of the title "Wild Rides"? Explain your thinking.*

News Scoop Edition (December 14, 2001)

A Nose for the Arts

Boon Yang likes to paint quickly, making long up-and-down streaks in bright colors. Bird prefers to brush deep blue and green across a canvas. People have compared their work to paintings by famous modern artists. But there's a *big* difference: Bird and Boon Yang hold a paintbrush with a trunk!

Boon Yang and Bird are two of about 100 elephants in Thailand and other Asian lands who have become successful artists. Their paintings have sold for as much as $2,200! Some even hang in museums.

Painting isn't the only kind of artwork done by Asian elephants. Some are making music too. A Thai elephant orchestra has recorded a CD. The money raised by selling CDs and paintings goes to an elephant-conservation center in Thailand.

Can Art Save Elephants?

Elephants in Thailand are in trouble. For years, they worked carrying heavy logs from rain forests. But the animals lost their jobs in 1989, when Thailand decided to protect the forests and stop logging. Some elephants wound up begging for food!

Artists Vitaly Komar and Alex Melamid wanted to help. They set up elephant art schools and brought attention to Thai elephants. Melamid says he's thrilled with the success of the project: "We've shown that anything is possible."

Overview *of* Week 2

Me First

by Helen Lester,
illustrated by
Lynn Munsinger
(Houghton Mifflin,
1992)

Synopsis

Pinkerton the pig
always manages to
be first until he rushes for
a sandwich and gets a surprise.

Alternative Books

- *The Magic Fish* by Freya Littledale
- *The Empty Pot* by Demi

Comprehension Focus

- Students *explore important ideas* in a story.
- Students *use inference* informally to think about what is important in a story.

Social Development Focus

- Students relate the value of fairness to their partner work.
- Students develop the group skills of giving reasons to support their thinking and sharing their partner time in a fair way.
- Students have a class meeting to discuss sharing their partner time fairly.

Materials

- "Class Meeting Ground Rules" chart

Day 1
Class Meeting

Lesson Purpose

Students:

▶ Review ground rules and procedures for a class meeting.

▶ Analyze the ways they have been interacting.

▶ Discuss sharing partner time in a fair way.

❶ GATHER FOR A CLASS MEETING

Tell the students that they are going to have a class meeting today to check in on how they are doing sharing their partner time in a fair way. If necessary, review the procedures and your expectations for how the students will move into a circle for the class meeting.

Have the pairs move into a circle. Briefly review the ground rules and remind the students to give reasons to support their own thinking.

> Class Meeting Ground Rules
> - One person talks at a time.

❷ CONDUCT THE CLASS MEETING

Ask the students to think about how they have worked with their partner and classmates over the past few weeks. Ask the following questions one at a time, giving the students time to think about each question. Then have the students discuss the questions, first in pairs, then as a class.

Think, Pair, Share

Q *I've noticed that sometimes when I call you back from partner work, both partners have not had a chance to share. Why does that happen?*

Q *What are some things you can do to make sure you share your partner time in a fair way?*

Q *Why is it important to make sure that both partners have time to share?*

Encourage the students to try some of their suggestions in the coming days, and plan to check in with them to see how they are doing.

▶ ADJOURN THE CLASS MEETING

Close the meeting by having the students briefly reflect on how they did following the ground rules. Adjourn the meeting and have the students return to their desks.

Individualized Daily Reading

▶ PRACTICE SELF-MONITORING

Have the students read books independently for up to 20 minutes.

Stop them at ten-minute intervals and have them monitor their comprehension by thinking about the questions on the "Think About Your Reading" chart.

As they read, circulate among them and ask individual students to read a selection aloud and tell you what it is about. Use the questions on the chart to help struggling students be aware of monitoring their own comprehension.

At the end of independent reading, have the students talk about using the questions on the chart to help them monitor their own comprehension.

Materials

• *Me First*

Day 2
Read-Aloud

Lesson Purpose

Students:

▶ Hear and discuss a story.

▶ *Visualize* part of a story.

▶ Give reasons to support their thinking.

▶ Share their partner time in a fair way.

▶ GET READY TO WORK TOGETHER

Have partners sit together. Tell the students that today they will hear and talk about a story. In the next lesson, they will hear the story again and talk about the important ideas in it.

Remind the students that in the last class meeting, they talked about ways to be fair during partner work. They will talk about how they did sharing their partner time at the end of the lesson.

▶ INTRODUCE *ME FIRST*

Show the cover of *Me First* and read the title and names of the author and illustrator aloud. Explain that this is a story about a pig named Pinkerton. Ask:

Q *What do you think this story might be about?*

Have two or three students share their thinking with the class. Ask for a show of hands in answer to the question:

Q *How many of you have ever wanted to be first?*

▶ READ *ME FIRST* ALOUD

Read *Me First* aloud, showing the illustrations as you read, and stopping as described below.

Suggested Vocabulary

plump: round or chubby (p. 3)

snouts: noses (p. 3)

trough-a-teria: (invented word) cafeteria (p. 5)

faint: not clear (p. 10)

in the distance: far away (p. 10)

pricked up: raised (p. 11)

trot: run slowly (p. 11)

smear: a thin layer (p. 12)

gallop: run fast (p. 14)

concerning: about (p. 29)

ELL Vocabulary

English Language Learners may benefit from discussing additional vocabulary, including:

right smack in front: right in front (p. 4)

picnic basket: a basket used to carry food for a meal outdoors (p. 9; refer to the illustration)

mayo: short for mayonaise (p. 12)

jiggled: shook (p. 16)

taking no notice: paying no attention (p. 18)

a few bends: a few turns on a road or path (p. 18)

tuck me in: put me in bed (p. 23)

scooted: ran along (p. 32)

Have the students close their eyes and ask them to visualize as you read pages 3 and 4 without showing the illustrations. Stop after:

> [p. 4] "'Me first!' he cried at story time, settling on his round bottom with his big head right smack in front of the book."

Ask:

Q *What picture of Pinkerton do you have in your mind?*

Have two or three students share their thinking with the class.

ELL Note

English language learners may benefit from previewing the book and discussing the difference between a *sandwich* and a *sandwitch* prior to the read-aloud. Explain the play on words and what it means to "...care for a sandwich"—one would like a sandwich to eat—and to actually "...care for a sandwitch"—to look after a witch from the sand.

Reread from the beginning of the book, showing the illustrations.

Stop after:

[p. 17] "'I am a Sandwitch, and I live in the sand, and you said you would care for a Sandwitch, so here I am. Care for me.'"

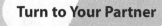

Turn to Your Partner

Have the students use "Turn to Your Partner" to discuss the following question. Remind them to use the partner time in a fair way. Ask:

Q *What has happened so far in the story? What do you think will happen next?*

Without sharing as a class, reread the last sentence on page 17 and continue reading to the end of the story.

▶ DISCUSS THE STORY AS A CLASS

Facilitate a whole-class discussion, using the following questions. Be ready to reread passages aloud and show illustrations again to help the students recall what they heard. Remind them to give reasons for their thinking.

Q *What happens in the story?*

Q *Would you want to be friends with Pinkerton? Why or why not?*

▶ REFLECT ON SHARING PARTNER TIME

Facilitate a brief discussion about how the students did using their partner time fairly. Share any observations you may have made.

Explain that in the next lesson the students will think about the important ideas in *Me First*.

Individualized Daily Reading

▶ READ INDEPENDENTLY/DOCUMENT IDR CONFERENCES

Have the students read independently for up to 20 minutes.

Use the "IDR Conference Notes" record sheet to conduct and document individual conferences. Continue to encourage the students to self–monitor as they read independently.

At the end of independent reading, have the students discuss their reading with their partner.

Materials

- *Me First*
- *Assessment Record Book*
- *Student Book,* IDR Journal section

Day 3
Strategy Lesson

Lesson Purpose

Students:

▸ Use inference informally to explore important ideas in a story.

▸ Give reasons to support their thinking.

▶ REVIEW EXPLORING IMPORTANT IDEAS

Have partners sit together. Explain that today the students will hear *Me First* read aloud again so that they can think about the important ideas in the story and the lesson they can learn from Pinkerton. Point out that authors sometimes use characters in a story to help readers think about important ideas or lessons about life.

▶ REREAD *ME FIRST*

Show the cover of *Me First* and reread the story aloud without stopping.

▶ DISCUSS THE IMPORTANT IDEAS

Facilitate a whole-class discussion about the story. If necessary, remind the students to give reasons for their thinking as they talk about their ideas. First in pairs, then as a class, discuss:

Turn to Your Partner

Q *What is Pinkerton like at the beginning of the story?*

Q *What is he like at the end of the story?*

Q *What is an important lesson that Pinkerton learns? Why is this an important idea for everyone to remember?*

Students might say:

❝ *Pinkerton learned that being first isn't always the best thing. I think this because in the story he tried to be first to get a sandwich and he ended up taking care of a sandwitch."*

❝ *I think that it is important for everyone to remember that you don't always have to be first. I think this because you need to take turns and be fair."*

Class Comprehension Assessment

Circulate as partners share. Ask yourself:

Q *Are the students able to identify the important lesson Pinkerton learns?*

Q *Are they able to use the text to support their thinking?*

Record your observations on page 27 of the *Assessment Record Book.*

Remind the students that stories often have messages or important lessons. Readers understand the message or lesson through what the characters say and do. Good readers think about important ideas and messages to help them make sense of a story. Explain that they will have more opportunities to think about important ideas as they hear and read stories.

Individualized Daily Reading

▶ DOCUMENT IDR CONFERENCES/ WRITE IN THE "IDR JOURNAL"

Have the students read independently for up to 20 minutes.

Use the "IDR Conference Notes" record sheet to conduct and document individual conferences. Continue to encourage the students to self-monitor as they read independently.

At the end of independent reading, have the students write about their reading in their "IDR Journal."

Overview *of* Week 3

Comprehension Focus

- Students *explore important ideas* in a story.

- Students *use inference* informally to think about what is important in a story.

Social Development Focus

- Students relate the value of fairness to their partner work.

- Students develop the group skill of giving reasons to support their thinking.

Big Al
y Andrew Clements,
lustrated by Yoshi
Aladdin, 1997)

Synopsis
A big, ugly
fish has trouble
making friends
because of his appearance,
until the day his scary appearance saves
them all from a fish net.

A Chair for My Mother*
by Vera B. Williams
Mulberry, 1982)

Synopsis
A girl, her
mother, and her
grandmother save
all their coins to buy an armchair
after their furniture is lost in a fire.
This book was also used in Unit 1, Week 4.

Alternative Books

- *You'll Grow Soon, Alex*
  by Andrea Shavick and Russell Ayto

- *Leo the Late Bloomer* by Robert Kraus

Materials

- *Big Al*

- "Reading Comprehension Strategies" chart

Day 1
Read-Aloud

Lesson Purpose

Students:

▶ Hear and discuss a story.

▶ Give reasons to support their thinking.

▶ Share their partner time in a fair way.

▶ ADD TO THE "READING COMPREHENSION STRATEGIES" CHART

Have partners sit together. Review that in the previous lesson they listened to a story and discussed the important ideas or lessons in it. In *Me First,* Pinkerton learned the important lesson that being first isn't always the best thing.

Refer to the "Reading Comprehension Strategies" chart. Write *exploring important ideas* on the chart. Remind the students that stories contain important things authors want readers to learn and remember. Sometimes the author doesn't tell the reader directly what the important idea or message is, and the reader has to use clues in the story to figure it out.

Explain that you will read another story today, and the students will continue to think about important ideas. Remind them to think about using their partner time fairly. Let them know that you will check in with them at the end of the lesson to see how they did.

▶ INTRODUCE *BIG AL*

Show the cover of *Big Al* and read the title and names of the author and illustrator. Explain that this is a story about a fish named Al. Ask the students to think about what happens to Al in the story.

Reading Comprehension
Strategies

- making connections

▶ READ *BIG AL* ALOUD

Read *Big Al* aloud, showing the illustrations and stopping as described below.

Suggested Vocabulary

seaweed: kind of plant that grows in the sea (p. 9)

disguise: clothing or covering that hides who you are (p. 9)

darted: moved suddenly and quickly (p. 15)

plowed: kept going (p. 15)

bulged: swelled (p. 18)

ELL Vocabulary

English Language Learners may benefit from discussing additional vocabulary, including:

steered clear: stayed away (p. 11)

in an instant: immediately (p. 16)

tangled: twisted together in a confused mass (p. 20)

captured: caught or trapped (p. 21)

fierce-looking: looking violent and dangerous (p. 25)

Read pages 2–15 aloud, and stop after:

> [p. 15] "Before he could even say 'Excuse me,' they were gone, and he was all alone again, sadder than ever."

Ask, and have the students use "Turn to Your Partner" to discuss: • • • • • **Turn to Your Partner**

Q *What do you know about Big Al so far?*

Q *What do you think will happen next?*

Have two or three students share their thinking with the class.

Reread the last sentence on page 15. Then continue reading to the end of the story.

▶ DISCUSS THE STORY AS A CLASS

Facilitate a whole-class discussion about the story. Be ready to reread passages aloud and show illustrations again to help the students recall what they heard. Remind them to give reasons for their thinking. Discuss questions such as:

Q *What is the problem in this story?*

Q *Why do you think Big Al has trouble making friends?*

Q *What are some things Big Al does to try to be friends with the little fish?*

Q *How is Big Al's problem solved at the end of the story?*

▶ REFLECT ON OUR PARTNER WORK

Facilitate a brief discussion about how the students did sharing their partner time in a fair way. Share any observations you may have made.

Explain that in the next lesson the students will have a chance to think about the important ideas in *Big Al*.

Individualized Daily Reading

▶ THINK ABOUT AND DISCUSS IMPORTANT IDEAS

Remind the students that they have been thinking about important ideas or messages in stories. Explain that today you want them to think about some important messages or ideas in the stories they are reading.

Have the students read independently for up to 20 minutes.

As the students read, circulate among them. Ask individual students questions such as:

Q *What is your book about?*

Q *What do you think the author wants us to think about or learn from this story?*

At the end of independent reading, have a few volunteers share what their book is about.

Materials

- *Big Al*

Day 2
Strategy Lesson

Lesson Purpose

Students:

▸ Use inference informally to explore important ideas.

▸ Give reasons to support their thinking.

▸ Share their partner time in a fair way.

▶ REVIEW *BIG AL*

Have partners sit together. Review that authors sometimes use characters' actions to give readers some important ideas to think about. Yesterday, they listened to *Big Al* and thought about what happens in the story. Today, they will hear *Big Al* again and discuss the important ideas in the story. Ask:

Q *What do you know about Big Al?*

Q *What do you know about the small fish?*

Have a few students share their thinking with the class.

▶ REREAD AND DISCUSS *BIG AL*

Show the cover of *Big Al* and explain that you will reread the story, stopping several times so that they can talk more about it. Remind the students to think about using their partner time fairly.

Reread the story aloud, without showing the illustrations, and stopping as indicated. You might want to show the illustration on the page where you stop before starting the discussion.

Stop after:

> [p. 12] "When the clouds of sand cleared away, all the other fish were gone."

Ask:

Q *What has happened in the story so far?*

Have a few students share their thinking with the class. Reread the last sentence on page 12 and continue. Stop after:

> [p. 15] "Before he could even say 'Excuse me,' they were gone, and he was all alone again, sadder than ever."

Ask:

Q *What are some words besides "sad" you could use to describe how Big Al feels in this part of the story?*

Have the students use "Turn to Your Partner" to discuss the question. Then have two or three students share their thinking with the class. Reread the last sentence and continue. Stop after:

> [p. 21] "How great to be free, but what a shame that the big fellow had been captured."

••••• **Turn to Your Partner**

Ask:

Q *How do the little fish feel in the part of the story I just read?*

Have the students use "Turn to Your Partner" to discuss the question. Then have two or three students share their thinking with the class. Reread the last sentence on page 21 and continue. Stop after:

> [p. 23] "Those fishermen took one look at him, and threw him right back into the ocean."

Ask:

Q *Why did the fishermen throw Big Al back in the water?*

Turn to Your Partner • • • • •

Have the students use "Turn to Your Partner" to discuss the question. Then have two or three students share their thinking with the class. Reread the last sentence on page 23 and continue reading to the end of the story.

❸ DISCUSS THE IMPORTANT IDEAS

Facilitate a whole-class discussion about the important ideas in the story. Remind the students to give reasons for their thinking. Discuss questions such as:

Q *What important lesson can we learn from Big Al and the small fish?*

Q *What do you think the author of this story is telling people about friendship?*

> ***Students mght say:***
>
> ❝ *I think the author is saying don't be afraid to be someone's friend just because they look scary. They might be nice like Big Al."*
>
> ❝ *I agree with [Nelda] and I think an important idea in this story is to help other people. The reason I think this is that Big Al tore the net to get the fish free."*
>
> ❝ *Don't judge someone by the outside, but by the inside. I think that because the little fish hurt Big Al's feelings."*

❹ REFLECT ON USING PARTNER TIME FAIRLY

Briefly discuss how partners did using the partner time fairly. Share your own observations and encourage the students to continue to think about working with each other in a fair way.

Individualized Daily Reading

5 READ INDEPENDENTLY/DOCUMENT IDR CONFERENCES

Ask the students to think about what their reading is about and an important idea in it. Have them read independently for up to 20 minutes.

Use the "IDR Conference Notes" record sheet to conduct and document individual conferences. Encourage the students to think about the important ideas in their reading.

At the end of independent reading, have the students read a part of their book that they think is important to their partner.

Materials

- *A Chair for My Mother* from Unit 1, Week 4

- *Student Book* pages 10–11

- "Reading Comprehension Strategies" chart

- *Assessment Record Book*

- *Student Book*, IDR Journal section

Day 3
Guided Strategy Practice

Lesson Purpose

Students:

▶ Use inference informally to explore important ideas.

▶ Give reasons to support their thinking.

▶ GET READY TO WORK TOGETHER

Have partners sit together. Remind the students that in the last few weeks, they have been focusing on sharing their partner time in a fair way. Ask:

Q *Why is it important for both partners to have time to share their thinking?*

Q *What are some things you have done to make sure both partners have time to talk?*

▶ REVISIT *A CHAIR FOR MY MOTHER* AND INTRODUCE THE EXCERPT

Explain that today the students will revisit a story that they heard at the beginning of the year. Show the cover of *A Chair for My Mother* and read the title and author's name. Ask:

Q *What do you remember about this story?*

Explain that you will read part of the story today, and they will talk about the important ideas in it.

Teacher Note

In this lesson, the students work with an excerpt from a familiar text to explore important ideas. If necessary, show the illustrations and summarize to help the students recall the story.

Have the students open their *Student Book* to page 10, and point out that this is an excerpt from *A Chair for My Mother*. This is the part of the story when the girl, her mother, and her grandmother move into their new apartment after the fire.

▶ READ THE EXCERPT ALOUD

Ask the students to follow along in their *Student Book* as you read pages 18–19 of *A Chair for My Mother* aloud. Explain that after they hear the excerpt, the students will talk about the important ideas in it and write their thinking on *Student Book* page 11.

Read pages 18–19 aloud, slowly and clearly. Stop after:

[p. 19] "'It's lucky we're young and can start all over.'"

Have the students use "Turn to Your Partner" to discuss:

Q   *What important message is the author telling us in this part of the story? Why do you think so?*

• • • • • **Turn to Your Partner**

Give pairs 5–7 minutes to talk and write about the important ideas in the excerpt.

Class Comprehension Assessment

Circulate among partners. Ask yourself:

Q   *Are the students able to determine the important ideas in the excerpt?*

Record your observations on page 28 of the *Assessment Record Book*.

▶ DISCUSS THE IMPORTANT IDEAS AS A CLASS

Facilitate a whole-class discussion using the following questions. Remind the students to give reasons to support their thinking.

Q *What are some important ideas you and your partner talked about?*

Q *What are some other important ideas in this story? What makes you think that?*

Reading Comprehension Strategies

– making connections

Refer to the "Reading Comprehension Strategies" chart and review that in this unit the students listened to stories and talked about important ideas or messages. Often one important idea in a story is a lesson about how we live and treat one another. Encourage the students to continue to think about important ideas in whatever they read.

▶ REFLECT ON WORKING TOGETHER

Have the students reflect on working together during this unit. Have them use "Think, Pair, Share" to discuss:

Think, Pair, Share

Q *How did your partner work go during this unit? What have you learned that will help you work with your next partner?*

Have a few partners share their ideas. Have the students take a minute to thank their partner.

Teacher Note

This is the last week of Unit 7. If you feel your students need more experience exploring important ideas before moving on, you may want to repeat this week's lessons with one of the alternative books listed on the Overview page. You will reassign partners for Unit 8.

Individualized Daily Reading

▶ WRITE ABOUT IMPORTANT IDEAS IN THE "IDR JOURNAL"

Explain that today you want the students to think about an important message or idea in the stories they are reading. At the end of independent reading, they will write about an important message in the book they are reading.

Have the students read independently for up to 20 minutes.

As the students read, circulate among them. Ask individual students questions such as:

Q *What is your book about?*

Q *What do you think the author wants us to think about or learn from this story?*

At the end of independent reading, have the students write about an important idea in their book.

Individual Student Assessment

Before continuing with Unit 8, take this opportunity to assess individual students' progress in identifying important ideas and messages. Please refer to pages 40–41 in the *Assessment Record Book* for instructions.

Social Skills Assessment

Take this opportunity to assess your students' social development using the Social Skills Assessment record sheet on pages 4–5 of the *Assessment Record Book*.

Unit 8 ▶ Revisiting the Reading Life

Unit 8 ▶ Revisiting the Reading Life

During this unit, the students reflect on the books they like and want to read. They answer questions to understand stories, and they think about the comprehension strategies they use to understand books. They analyze the effect of their behavior on others and on the group work. They also develop the group skills of giving reasons to support their thinking and sharing their partner time in a fair way. They participate in a class meeting to discuss what they liked about their reading community.

Week 1 ▶ *little blue and little yellow*
by Leo Lionni

Overview *of* Week 1

**ttle blue and
ttle yellow**

Leo Lionni
HarperCollins, 1959)

ynopsis
This is the story of
blue dot and a
ellow dot that
re best friends,
nd what happens to them
hen they
ug each other.

Alternative Books

- *Dear Juno* by Soyung Pak
- *Cornelius* by Leo Lionni

Comprehension Focus

- Students answer questions to understand stories.

- Students reflect on books and stories they like and want to read.

- Students think about the comprehension strategies they use to understand books.

Social Development Focus

- Students analyze the effect of their behavior on others and on the group work.

- Students develop the group skills of giving reasons to support their thinking and sharing their partner time in a fair way.

- Students participate in a class meeting to discuss what they liked about their reading community.

▶ Do Ahead

- Collect one read-aloud book from each unit in the *Making Meaning* program. Choose fiction and nonfiction that the students enjoyed (see Day 2, Step 1 on page 330).

- Prepare a chart with the title "Kinds of Books We Like" (see Day 2, Step 2 on pages 330–331).

Materials

- *little blue and little yellow*
- "Reading Comprehension Strategies" chart

Day 1
Read-Aloud

Lesson Purpose

Students:

▶ Begin working with a new partner.

▶ Hear and discuss a story.

▶ Think about the reading comprehension strategies they use.

▶ Give reasons to support their thinking.

About Revisiting the Reading Life

The purpose of this unit is to help the students reflect on the reading work they have done in the *Making Meaning* program and the strategies they have learned to help them understand what they read. This week they will think about the books they like, and reflect on their reading community.

Have all the *Making Meaning* program books and other books you read aloud available for Individualized Daily Reading and the lesson extensions. Select seven or more of these books to use on Day 2.

❶ PAIR STUDENTS AND GET READY TO WORK TOGETHER

Randomly assign partners and have them sit together. Tell the students that this week they will think about books they like and their reading community. Today, they will talk about the strategies they learned to help them understand what they read. They will also hear a new story.

❷ REVIEW THE "READING COMPREHENSION STRATEGIES" CHART

Remind the students that they practiced several strategies this year that helped them understand their reading. Refer to the "Reading Comprehension Strategies" chart and briefly review each strategy.

Teacher Note

As you mention each strategy, you might show the class a book and connect the book to the strategy. (For example, "When you listened to 'The Kite' from *Days with Frog and Toad* you visualized to get a picture in your mind of what was happening in the story.")

Tell the students that you would like them to think about the comprehension strategies they are using as they listen to today's read-aloud.

▶ INTRODUCE *LITTLE BLUE AND LITTLE YELLOW*

Show the cover of *little blue and little yellow* and read the title and name of the author aloud. Explain that this is a story about a friendship between two dots, a blue one and a yellow one.

Remind the students that as they listen to the story you want them to think about the strategies they are using to help them understand it.

▶ READ *LITTLE BLUE AND LITTLE YELLOW* ALOUD

Read *little blue and little yellow* aloud, showing the illustrations and stopping as described below.

Suggested Vocabulary

> **tunnel:** a passage built under the ground (p. 23)

> **ELL Vocabulary**
> English Language Learners may benefit from discussing additional vocabulary, including:
>
> *Hide-and-Seek:* a game in which players hide while one person ("it") looks for them (p. 8)
> *Ring-a-Ring-O'Roses:* a game in which players sing and walk in a circle (p. 9)
> **chased:** ran after (p. 24)
> **pulled themselves together:** stopped crying (p. 32)

Read pages 3–21 aloud, and stop after:

[p. 21] "…until they were green."

Ask, and have the students use "Turn to Your Partner" to discuss: • • • • •   **Turn to Your Partner**

Q *What has happened in the story so far?*

Have a few volunteers briefly share their thinking.

Reread the lines on pages 20 and 21; then continue reading to the end of the story.

Turn to Your Partner

5 DISCUSS THE STORY

First in pairs, then as a class, discuss the following questions. Remind the students to give reasons for their thinking.

Q *What happens to little blue and little yellow?*

Q *What can we learn about friendship from this story?*

> **Students might say:**
> " *You can have a friend who is different than you.*"
> " *It doesn't matter if you're different from your friend.*"
> " *Friends stick together.*"

Q *Which comprehension strategy did you use as you listened to the story? When did you use [wondering]?*

6 REFLECT ON WORKING TOGETHER

Facilitate a brief discussion about how the students interacted during the read-aloud and discussion. Ask partners to tell each other one thing they liked about how they worked together. Have a few students share their partner's idea.

Individualized Daily Reading

7 PRACTICE SELF-MONITORING

Direct the students' attention to the "Think About Your Reading" chart and remind them that stopping and thinking about the questions on the chart helps them keep track of how well they are understanding their reading. Read the charted questions and tell them that they will practice this procedure again today.

Have the students read independently for up to 20 minutes.

Stop them at five-minute intervals. At each stop, read the questions on the chart and have them think about each one.

As they read, circulate among them and ask individual students to tell you what their book is about. Encourage them to think about the charted questions.

At the end of independent reading, have the students share their reading either with a partner or as a class.

Extensions

▶ 8 REVISIT READ-ALOUDS
Give pairs time to read, retell, and talk about books you have read aloud this year. Make time each day for pairs to share a book briefly, together or with another pair.

▶ 9 SHARE PERSONAL FAVORITES
Have the students share a favorite book from home or school with their partner or the class. Have the students talk about why they like the book or their favorite part or show an illustration.

Materials

- Read-aloud books from this year, selected ahead

- "Kinds of Books We Like" chart, prepared ahead, and a marker

- *Student Book* page 12

Day 2
Reflect on Reading Lives

Lesson Purpose

Students:

▶ Discuss the kinds of stories they like to read.

▶ Share partner time in a fair way.

❶ REVIEW FAMILIAR BOOKS

Have partners sit together. Tell them that today they will think about the kinds of stories they like and want to read this summer.

Direct their attention to the read-aloud books you selected from the year. Explain that these are some of the books they heard or read this year. Remind them that some of these books are fiction (about imaginary people and events) and some are nonfiction (about real people, events, or things). If necessary, give a brief summary of each of the books you selected.

❷ DISCUSS FAVORITE KINDS OF BOOKS

Think, Pair, Share

Have the students use "Think, Pair, Share" to talk about the selected books and the kinds of books they like. Remind them to focus on sharing their partner time in a fair way. Ask:

Q *Which of these books did you enjoy the most? Why did you like that book?*

Q *What kinds of books do you like to read? Why do you like to read these books?*

Teacher Note
If the students have difficulty categorizing the kinds the books they like, point out some they heard or read this year. For example, animal stories (*McDuff Moves In, The Tale of Peter Rabbit*), true stories (*Ibis: A True Whale Story*), books about science (*Plants That Eat Animals*), funny stories (*Alexander and the Terrible, Horrible, No Good, Very Bad Day*), and stories that teach a lesson (*Me First*).

Students might say:

❝ *I like true stories because you learn about real people like astronauts.*❞

❝ *I like funny stories like Captain Underpants because they make me laugh.*❞

❝ *I like the Magic School Bus stories because I like reading about science.*❞

As the students share their ideas, record them on the "Kinds of Books We Like" chart.

❸ **WRITE ABOUT SUMMER READING**

Ask the students to open their *Student Book* to page 12, "Thoughts About My Reading Life." Read the title and explain that the students will write about the kinds of books and stories they want to read this summer and where they think they will do their summer reading. Later they will share their thoughts with their classmates.

Read the first question on *Student Book* page 12 and have the students individually write their answer to the question. Follow the same procedure for the second question.

As the students work, circulate among them. Probe the students' thinking with questions such as:

Q *What kinds of stories do you like to read or listen to? Why do you like that kind of story?*

Q *Do you like books about real things? What kinds of things do you want to learn about?*

Q *I plan to [sit outside in my backyard] to do my summer reading. Where can you picture yourself reading this summer?*

◢ 4 SHARE THOUGHTS ABOUT SUMMER READING

Explain that partners will talk about what they wrote on *Student Book* page 12. Give pairs time to talk; then facilitate a brief whole-class discussion by asking:

Q *What kinds of books and stories do you want to read this summer? Why?*

Q *Where do you think you might want to read a book this summer?*

Q *Who wants to read [the same/different] kinds of books as [Aiden] wants to read?*

◢ 5 DISCUSS PARTNER WORK

Briefly discuss how partners did sharing the partner time in a fair way. Explain that in the next lesson the students will talk about what they liked about their reading community this year.

Individualized Daily Reading

◢ 6 REVISIT THE STUDENTS' READING LIVES

Have the students read independently for up to 20 minutes.

As they read, circulate among them and talk to individual students about their reading lives. To guide your discussion, use what they have written on *Student Book* page 12 or questions such as:

Q *What is one of your favorite books to read? Why do you like that book?*

Q *What kinds of books do you like to read? Do you prefer fiction or nonfiction books? Why?*

Q   *What do you want to read this summer? What would you like to read next year?*

Q   *What do you like about reading?*

At the end of independent reading, give the students a few minutes to share what they read either with a partner or as a class.

Extensions

▷ REVISIT READ-ALOUDS

Give pairs time to read, retell, and talk about books you have read aloud this year. Make time each day for pairs to briefly share a book together or with another pair.

▷ SHARE PERSONAL FAVORITES

Have students share a favorite book from home or school with the class. Have the students talk about why they like the book or their favorite part or show an illustration.

Materials

- "Our Class Norms" chart
- "Class Meeting Ground Rules" chart
- *Student Book* page 13
- *Student Book,* IDR Journal section

Day 3
Reflection and Class Meeting

Lesson Purpose

Students:

▶ Check in on the class norms.

▶ Reflect on and write about how they worked together in a community.

▌ GET READY TO THINK ABOUT THE READING COMMUNITY

Have partners sit together. Remind them that yesterday they talked about books they liked and thought about their summer reading. Today they will think about how they worked together this year as a reading community. They will discuss their class norms and talk and write about what they liked about their community.

Our Class Norms

- We will talk nicely to each other.

Think, Pair, Share

▌ DISCUSS HOW THE STUDENTS LIVED BY THE CLASS NORMS

Direct the students' attention to the "Our Class Norms" chart and briefly review the norms. For each question below, have the students close their eyes and think quietly for a moment before talking to their partner. After partners have talked, have a few volunteers share their thinking with the class. Ask:

Q *Why did we set up these norms in our classroom?*

Q *How do you think we did this year living by our norms? Why do you think that?*

Q *When did we [talk nicely to each other]?*

Teacher Note

The purpose of the last question is to encourage the students to think of concrete examples of ways they put the class norms into practice.

▶ DRAW AND WRITE ABOUT THE READING COMMUNITY

Ask the students to turn to *Student Book* page 13, "What I Liked About Our Reading Community." Explain that they will draw a picture and write about what they liked about their community. They will share their pictures and writing later at a class meeting.

Have the students complete their *Student Book* page.

▶ GATHER FOR A CLASS MEETING

When most students have finished drawing and writing, have them bring their *Student Book* and come to the circle, with partners sitting together. Make sure the students can see one another.

Briefly review the "Class Meeting Ground Rules" chart.

▶ CONDUCT THE CLASS MEETING

Explain that the purpose of the class meeting is to share what the students drew and wrote about what they liked about their reading community. Have partners share their *Student Book* pages with each other. Remind them to share the partner time in a fair way.

After partners have talked, have a few volunteers share their drawing and writing with the class. Facilitate a discussion by asking:

Q *Did you or your partner write something similar to what [Joslyn] wrote? Share it with us.*

Q *Who drew and wrote an idea that is different from [Joslyn's]? Share it with us.*

Q *What question do you want to ask [Joslyn] about what she shared?*

Teacher Note

As the students work, circulate among them. If the students have difficulty thinking of ideas, probe their thinking with questions such as:

Q *What did you like about working with a partner?*

Q *What was helpful when you were listening to books?*

Q *In what ways were students kind and caring during independent reading time?*

Class Meeting Ground Rules
- One person talks at a time.

Teacher Note

You may want to hold the class meeting later in the day or on the following day.

6 REFLECT ON THE CLASS MEETING

Briefly discuss how the students did following the ground rules during the class meeting; then have the students return to their desks or tables.

Individualized Daily Reading

7 REVISIT THE STUDENTS' READING LIVES/ WRITE IN THE "IDR JOURNAL"

Have the students read independently for up to 20 minutes.

As they read, circulate among them and talk to individual students about their reading lives. To guide your discussion, use what they have written on *Student Book* page 12 or questions such as:

Q *What is one of your favorite books to read? Why do you like that book?*

Q *What kinds of books do you like to read? Do you prefer fiction or nonfiction books?*

Q *What do you want to read this summer? What would you like to read next year?*

Q *What do you like about reading?*

At the end of independent reading, have the students write in their "IDR Journal" about what they like about the book they read.

Extension

▶ VISIT THE COMMUNITY LIBRARY

If possible, arrange a visit to the community library. Check with the librarian about the procedures for obtaining a library card. Familiarize the students with the library, and encourage them to go to the library to borrow books to read during their summer break.

Appendices

Grade 2
Sample Calendar

Note: Your school year may be different from this calendar. Lessons can take place on any three days of the week.

SEPTEMBER

M	T	W	Th	F
Unit 1: The Reading Life **Week 1** ▶				
Week 2 ▶				
Week 3 ▶				

OCTOBER

M	T	W	Th	F
Week 4 ▶				
Break				
Unit 2: Making Connections **Week 1** ▶				
Week 2 ▶				

NOVEMBER

M	T	W	Th	F
Unit 3: Visualizing **Week 1** ▶				
Week 2 ▶				
Week 3 ▶				
Week 4 ▶				

DECEMBER

M	T	W	Th	F
IDR Conference Week				
Break				
Break				
Break				

JANUARY

M	T	W	Th	F
Unit 4: Making Inferences About Characters **Week 1** ▶				
Week 2 ▶				
Week 3 ▶				
Week 4 ▶				

FEBRUARY

M	T	W	Th	F
Break				
Unit 5: Exploring Fiction **Week 1** ▶				
Week 2 ▶				
Week 3 ▶				

MARCH

M	T	W	Th	F
Break				
Unit 6: Exploring Nonfiction **Week 1** ▶				
Week 2 ▶				
Week 3 ▶				

APRIL

M	T	W	Th	F
Week 4 ▶				
Week 5 ▶				
IDR Conference Week				
Break				

MAY

M	T	W	Th	F
Unit 7: Exploring Important Ideas **Week 1** ▶				
Week 2 ▶				
Week 3 ▶				
Unit 8: Revisiting the Reading Life **Week 1** ▶				

Grade 2

	Lesson	Title	Author	Form	Genre/Type
Unit 1	▶ Week 1	*McDuff Moves In*	Rosemary Wells	picture book	fiction
		Poppleton: "The Library"	Cynthia Rylant	picture book	fiction
	▶ Week 2	*Sheila Rae, the Brave*	Kevin Henkes	picture book	fiction
	▶ Week 3	*Ibis: A True Whale Story*	John Himmelman	picture book	fiction
	▶ Week 4	*A Chair for My Mother*	Vera B. Williams	picture book	realistic fiction
Unit 2	▶ Week 1	*Jamaica Tag-Along*	Juanita Havill	picture book	realistic fiction
	▶ Week 2	*Alexander and the Terrible, Horrible, No Good, Very Bad Day*	Judith Viorst	picture book	fiction
Unit 3	▶ Week 1	*A Tree Is Nice*	Janice May Udry	picture book	poetic nonfiction
		Fathers, Mothers, Sisters, Brothers: A Collection of Family Poems: "My Baby Brother"	Mary Ann Hoberman	picture book	poetry
	▶ Week 2	*Poppleton and Friends:* "Dry Skin"	Cynthia Rylant	picture book	fiction
		Days with Frog and Toad: "The Kite"	Arnold Lobel	picture book	fiction
	▶ Week 3	*The Paperboy*	Dav Pilkey	picture book	realistic fiction
Unit 4	▶ Week 1	*What Mary Jo Shared*	Janice May Udry	picture book	realistic fiction
	▶ Week 2	*Erandi's Braids*	Antonio Hernández Madrigal	picture book	realistic fiction
	▶ Week 3	*Chester's Way*	Kevin Henkes	picture book	fiction
	▶ Week 4	*The Greatest Treasure*	Demi	picture book	folktale
Unit 5	▶ Week 1	*The Incredible Painting of Felix Clousseau*	Jon Agee	picture book	fiction
		The Ghost-Eye Tree	Bill Martin, Jr. and John Archambault	picture book	realistic fiction
	▶ Week 2	*Galimoto*	Karen Lynn Williams	picture book	realistic fiction
	▶ Week 3	*The Paper Crane*	Molly Bang	picture book	fiction
Unit 6	▶ Week 1	*The Tale of Peter Rabbit*	Beatrix Potter	picture book	fiction
		Beatrix Potter	Alexandra Wallner	picture book	narrative nonfiction: biography
	▶ Week 2	*The Art Lesson*	Tomie dePaola	picture book	fiction
		"Draw, Draw, Draw": A Short Biography of Tomie dePaola	Robyn Raymer	article	narrative nonfiction
	▶ Week 3	*It Could Still Be a Worm*	Allan Fowler	picture book	expository nonfiction
		Plants that Eat Animals	Allan Fowler	picture book	expository nonfiction
	▶ Week 4	*Fishes: A True Book*	Melissa Stewart	picture book	expository nonfiction
	▶ Week 5	*POP! A Book About Bubbles*	Kimberly Brubaker Bradley	picture book	expository nonfiction
Unit 7	▶ Week 1	"Wild Rides"	Lev Grossman	article	expository nonfiction
		"Summer of the Shark"		article	expository nonfiction
		"A Nose for the Arts"		article	expository nonfiction
	▶ Week 2	*Me First*	Helen Lester	picture book	fiction
	▶ Week 3	*Big Al*	Andrew Clements	picture book	fiction
Unit 8	▶ Week 1	*little yellow and little blue*	Leo Lionni	picture book	fiction

Grade K

Brave Bear	Kathy Mallat
Cat's Colors	Jane Cabrera
"Charlie Needs a Cloak"	Tomie dePaola
Cookie's Week	Cindy Ward
Corduroy	Don Freeman
A Day with a Doctor	Jan Kottke
A Day with a Mail Carrier	Jan Kottke
Flower Garden	Eve Bunting
Harry the Dirty Dog	Gene Zion
I Want To Be a Vet	Dan Liebman
I Was So Mad	Mercer Mayer
If You Give a Mouse a Cookie	Laura Joffe Numeroff
The Kissing Hand	Audrey Penn
Knowing About Noses	Allan Fowler
A Letter to Amy	Ezra Jack Keats
Maisy's Pool	Lucy Cousins
My Friends	Taro Gomi
Noisy Nora	Rosemary Wells
A Porcupine Named Fluffy	Helen Lester
Pumpkin Pumpkin	Jeanne Titherington
A Tiger Cub Grows Up	Joan Hewett
When Sophie Gets Angry— Really, Really Angry	Molly Bang
Whistle for Willie	Ezra Jack Keats
White Rabbit's Color Book	Alan Baker
Working Dogs	Sherry Shahan

Grade 1

Best Friends Sleep Over	Jacqueline Rogers
Caps for Sale	Esphyr Slobodkina
Charlie Anderson	Barbara Abercrombie
Chrysanthemum	Kevin Henkes
Curious George Goes to an Ice Cream Shop	Margret Rey and Alan J. Shalleck
Did You See What I Saw? Poems About School	Kay Winters
Down the Road	Alice Schertle
An Extraordinary Egg	Leo Lionni
Feeding Time at the Zoo	Sherry Shahan
A Harbor Seal Pup Grows Up	Joan Hewett
In the Tall, Tall Grass	Denise Fleming
Is Your Mama a Llama?	Deborah Guarino
It's Mine!	Leo Lionni
Julius	Angela Johnson
A Kangaroo Joey Grows Up	Joan Hewett
Little Nino's Pizzeria	Karen Barbour
A Look at Teeth	Allan Fowler
Matthew and Tilly	Rebecca C. Jones
McDuff and the Baby	Rosemary Wells
Peter's Chair	Ezra Jack Keats
Quick as a Cricket	Audrey Wood
Raptors!	Lisa McCourt
Sheep Out to Eat	Nancy Shaw
The Snowy Day	Ezra Jack Keats
Throw Your Tooth on the Roof	Selby B. Beeler
The Trip	Ezra Jack Keats
When I Was Little	Jamie Lee Curtis

Grade 3

Alexander, Who's Not	Judith Viorst
(Do you hear me? I mean it) Going To Move	
Aunt Flossie's Hats (and Crab Cakes Later)	Elizabeth Fitzgerald
Bashi, Elephant Baby	Theresa Radcliffe
Boundless Grace	Mary Hoffman
Brave Harriet	Marissa Moss
Brave Irene	William Steig
Cherries and Cherry Pits	Vera B. Williams
City Green	DyAnne DiSalvo-Ryan
A Day's Work	Eve Bunting
Fables	Arnold Lobel
Flashy Fantastic Rain Forest Frogs	Dorothy Hinshaw Patent
The Girl Who Loved Wild Horses	Paul Goble
Have You Seen Bugs?	Joanne Oppenheim
I Can Read About Planets	Darrow Schecter
Julius, the Baby of the World	Kevin Henkes
Keepers	Jeri Hanel Watts
Knots on a Counting Rope	Bill Martin, Jr. and John Archambault
Let's Eat!	Ana Zamorano
Lifetimes	David L. Rice
Mailing May	Michael O. Tunnell
Miss Nelson Is Missing!	Harry Allard and James Marshall
Officer Buckle and Gloria	Peggy Rathmann
The Paper Bag Princess	Robert N. Munsch
The Patchwork Quilt	Valerie Flournoy
Reptiles: A True Book	Melissa Stewart
What is a Bat?	Bobbie Kalman and Heather Levigne
Wilma Unlimited: How Wilma Rudolph	Kathleen Krull
Became the World's Fastest Woman	

Grade 4

Amelia's Road	Linda Jacobs Altman
Animal Senses	Pamela Hickman
Babushka Baba Yaga	Patricia Polacco
A Bad Case of Stripes	David Shannon
Basket Moon	Mary Lyn Ray
The Bat Boy & His Violin	Gavin Curtis
Chicken Sunday	Patricia Polacco
Coming to America	Betsy Maestro
Digging Up Tyrannosaurus Rex	John R. Horner and Don Lessem
The Dragon Takes a Wife	Walter Dean Myers
Flight	Robert Burleigh
Home Place	Crescent Dragonwagon
Hurricane	David Wiesner
In My Own Backyard	Judi Kurjian
The Memory Coat	Elvira Woodruff
Mirette on the High Wire	Emily Arnold McCully
My Man Blue	Nikki Grimes
The Old Woman Who Named Things	Cynthia Rylant
Peppe the Lamplighter	Elisa Bartone
A Picture Book of Amelia Earhart	David A. Adler
A Picture Book of Harriet Tubman	David A. Adler
A Picture Book of Rosa Parks	David A. Adler
Sami and the Time of the Troubles	Florence Parry Heide and Judith Heide Gilliland
Slinky, Scaly, Slithery Snakes	Dorothy Hinshaw Patent
Song and Dance Man	Karen Ackerman
Teammates	Peter Golenbock
Thunder Cake	Patricia Polacco

Grade 5

A Band of Angels	Deborah Hopkinson
Big Cats	Seymour Simon
The Circuit: Stories from the Life of a Migrant Child	Francisco Jiménez
Earthquakes	Seymour Simon
Everybody Cooks Rice	Norah Dooley
Harry Houdini: Master of Magic	Robert Kraske
Hey World, Here I Am!	Jean Little
Letting Swift River Go	Jane Yolen
Life in the Rain Forests	Lucy Baker
The Lotus Seed	Sherry Garland
Mufaro's Beautiful Daughters: An African Tale	John Steptoe
A Picture Book of Jesse Owens	David A. Adler
Richard Wright and the Library Card	William Miller
A River Ran Wild	Lynne Cherry
Something to Remember Me By	Susan V. Bosak
Star of Fear, Star of Hope	Jo Hoestlandt
The Summer My Father Was Ten	Pat Brisson
True Stories of Heroes	Paul Dowswell
Uncle Jed's Barbershop	Margaree King Mitchell
The Van Gogh Cafe	Cynthia Rylant
Wildfires	Seymour Simon

Grade 6

America Street: *A Multicultural Anthology of Stories*	Anne Mazer
And Still the Turtle Watched	Sheila MacGill-Callahan
Baseball Saved Us	Ken Mochizuki
Chato's Kitchen	Gary Soto
Coming Home	Floyd Cooper
Dear Benjamin Banneker	Andrea Davis Pinkney
Encounter	Jane Yolen
Every Living Thing	Cynthia Rylant
Life in the Oceans	Lucy Baker
New Kids in Town	Janet Bode
Science Fiction Stories	Edward Blishen
Sweet Clara and the Freedom Quilt	Deborah Hopkinson
Thank You, Mr. Falker	Patricia Polacco
Train to Somewhere	Eve Bunting
True Mystery Stories	Finn Bevan
Voices from the Fields	S. Beth Atkin
Volcano	Patricia Lauber
Whales	Seymour Simon
Why Don't You Get a Horse, Sam Adams?	Jean Fritz
Why Mosquitoes Buzz In People's Ears	Verna Aardema

Bibliography

Anderson, Richard C., Elfrieda H. Hiebert, Judith A. Scott, and Ian A. G. Wilkinson. *Becoming a Nation of Readers: The Report of the Commission on Reading*. Washington, DC: The National Institute of Education, 1985.

Anderson, Richard C., and P. David Pearson. "A Schema-Theoretic View of Basic Process in Reading Comprehension." In *Handbook of Reading Research*, P. David Pearson (ed.). New York: Longman, 1984.

Armbruster, Bonnie B., Fred Lehr, and Jean Osborn. *Put Reading First: The Research Building Blocks for Teaching Children to Read*. Jessup, MD: National Institute for Literacy, 2001.

Beck, Isabel L., and Margaret G. McKeown. "Text Talk: Capturing the Benefits of Read-Aloud Experiences for Young Children." *The Reading Teacher* 55:1 (2001): 10–19.

Block, C. C., and M. Pressley. *Comprehension Instruction: Research-Based Best Practices*. New York: Guilford Press, 2001.

Calkins, Lucy M. *The Art of Teaching Reading*. New York: Addison-Wesley Longman, 2001.

Contestable, Julie W., Shaila Regan, Susie Alldredge, Carol Westrich, and Laurel Robertson. *Number Power: A Cooperative Approach to Mathematics and Social Development Grades K–6*. Oakland, CA: Developmental Studies Center, 1999.

Cunningham, Anne E., and Keith E. Stanovich. "What Reading Does for the Mind." *American Educator* Spring/Summer (1998): 8–15.

Developmental Studies Center. *Blueprints for a Collaborative Classroom*. Oakland, CA: Developmental Studies Center, 1997.

_____. *Ways We Want Our Class To Be*. Oakland, CA: Developmental Studies Center, 1996.

DeVries, Rheta, and Betty Zan. *Moral Classrooms, Moral Children*. New York: Teachers' College Press, 1994.

Dewey, J. *Democracy and Education*. New York: Macmillan, 1916.

Farstrup, Alan E., and S. Jay Samuels. *What Research Has to Say About Reading Instruction*. 3rd Ed. Newark, DE: International Reading Association, 2002.

Fielding, Linda G., and P. David Pearson. "Reading Comprehension: What Works." *Educational Leadership* 51:5 (1994): 1–11.

Gambrell, Linda B., Lesley Mandel Morrow, Susan B. Neuman, and Michael Pressley, eds. *Best Practices in Literacy Instruction*. New York: Guilford Press, 1999.

Harvey, Stephanie. *Nonfiction Matters: Reading, Writing, and Research in Grades 3–8*. York, ME: Stenhouse Publishers, 1998.

Harvey, Stephanie, and Anne Goudvis. *Strategies That Work: Teaching Comprehension to Enhance Understanding*. York, ME: Stenhouse Publishers, 2000.

Harvey, Stephanie, Sheila McAuliffe, Laura Benson, Wendy Cameron, Sue Kempton, Pat Lusche, Debbie Miller, Joan Schroeder, and Julie Weaver. "Teacher-Researchers Study the Process of Synthesizing in Six Primary Classrooms." *Language Arts* 73 (1996): 564–574.

International Reading Association. "What Is Evidence-Based Reading Instruction? A Position Statement of the International Reading Association." Newark, DE: International Reading Association, 2002.

Johnson, David W., Roger T. Johnson, and Edythe Johnson Holubec. *The New Circles of Learning: Cooperation in the Classroom*. Alexandria, VA: Association for Supervision and Curriculum Development, 1994.

Kagan, Spencer. *Cooperative Learning*. San Juan Capistrano, CA: Resources of Teachers, 1992.

Kamil, Michael L., Peter B. Mosenthal, P. David Pearson, and Rebecca Barr, eds. *Handbook of Reading Research, Volume III*. Mahwah, NJ: Lawrence Erlbaum Associates, 2000.

Keene, Ellin O., and Susan Zimmermann. *Mosaic of Thought: Teaching Comprehension in a Reader's Workshop*. Portsmouth, NH: Heinemann, 1997.

Kohlberg, Lawrence. *The Psychology of Moral Development*. New York: Harper and Row, 1984.

Kohn, Alfie. *Beyond Discipline: From Compliance to Community*. Association for Supervision and Curriculum Development, 1996.

Kohn, Alfie. *Punished by Rewards: The Trouble with Gold Stars, Incentive Plans, A's, Praise, and Other Bribes*. New York: Houghton Mifflin Company, 1999.

NEA Task Force on Reading. *Report of the NEA Task Force on Reading 2000.*

Nucci, Larry P., ed. *Moral Development and Character Education: A Dialogue*. Berkeley, CA: McCutchan Publishing Corporation, 1989.

Optiz, Michael F., ed. *Literacy Instruction for Culturally and Linguistically Diverse Students*. Newark, DE: International Reading Association, 1998.

Pearson, P. David, J. A. Dole, G. G. Duffy, and L. R. Roehler. "Developing Expertise in Reading Comprehension: What Should Be Taught and How Should It Be Taught?" In *What Research Has to Say to the Teacher of Reading*, J. Farstup and S. J. Samuels (eds.). Newark, DE: International Reading Association, 1992.

Piaget, Jean. *The Child's Conception of the World*. Trans. Joan and Andrew Tomlinson. Lanham, MD: Littlefield Adams, 1969.

Piaget, Jean. *The Moral Judgment of the Child*. Trans. Marjorie Gabain. New York: The Free Press, 1965.

Pinnell, Gay Su, and Irene C. Fountas. *Leveled Books for Readers Grade 3–6*. Portsmouth, NH: Heinemann, 2002.

_____. *Matching Books to Readers: Using Leveled Books in Guided Reading, K–3*. Portsmouth, NH: Heinemann, 1999.

Pressley, Michael. *Effective Beginning Reading Instruction: The Rest of the Story from Research*. National Education Association, 2002.

Pressley, Michael. *Reading Instruction That Works*. New York: Guilford Press, 1998.

Pressley, Michael, Janice Almasi, Ted Schuder, Janet Bergman, Sheri Hite, Pamela B. El-Dinary, and Rachel Brown. "Transactional Instruction of Comprehension Strategies: The Montgomery County, Maryland, SAIL Program." *Reading and Writing Quarterly: Overcoming Learning Difficulties* 10 (1994): 5–19.

Routman, Regie. *Reading Essentials: The Specifics You Need to Teach Reading Well*. Portsmouth, NH: Heinemann, 2003.

Serafini, Frank. *The Reading Workshop: Creating Space for Readers*. Portsmouth, NH: Heinemann, 2001.

Taylor, Barbara M., Michael Pressley, and P. David Pearson. *Research-Supported Characteristics of Teachers and Schools That Promote Reading Achievement*. National Education Association, 2002.

Trelease, Jim. *The Read-Aloud Handbook*. New York: Penguin Books, 1995.

Weaver, Brenda M. *Leveling Books K–6: Matching Readers to Text*. Newark, DE: International Reading Association, 2000.

Williams, Joan A. "Classroom Conversations: Opportunities to Learn for ESL Students in Mainstream Classrooms." *The Reading Teacher* 54:8 (2001): 750–757.

Making Meaning™

Reorder Information

Kindergarten

Complete Classroom Package   MMGSK0

Contents: Teacher's Manual, Orientation Handbook and videos, 24 trade books

Available separately

Classroom Materials without Trade Books	MMTPK0
Teacher's Manual	MMTMK0
Trade Book Set (24 books)	MMBSK0

Grade 1

Complete Classroom Package   MMGS10

Contents: Teacher's Manual, Orientation Handbook and videos, Class Set (25 Student Books, Assessment Record Book), 27 trade books

Available separately

Classroom Materials without Trade Books	MMTP10
Teacher's Manual	MMTM10
Replacement Class Set (25/1)	MMCS10
Student Book Pack (5 books)	MMSS10
Assessment Record Book	MMAB10
Trade Book Set (27 books)	MMBS10

Grade 2

Complete Classroom Package   MMGS20

Contents: Teacher's Manual (2 volumes), Orientation Handbook and videos, Class Set (25 Student Books, Assessment Record Book), 30 trade books

Available separately

Classroom Materials without Trade Books	MMTP20
Teacher's Manual, vol. 1	MMTM20
Teacher's Manual, vol. 2	MMTM21
Replacement Class Set (25/1)	MMCS20
Student Book Pack (5 books)	MMSS20
Assessment Record Book	MMAB20
Trade Book Set (30 books)	MMBS20

Grade 3

Complete Classroom Package   MMGS30

Contents: Teacher's Manual (2 volumes), Orientation Handbook and videos, Class Set (25 Student Books, Assessment Record Book), 27 trade books

Available separately

Classroom Materials without Trade Books	MMTP30
Teacher's Manual, vol. 1	MMTM30
Teacher's Manual, vol. 2	MMTM31
Replacement Class Set (25/1)	MMCS30
Student Book Pack (5 books)	MMSS30
Assessment Record Book	MMAB30
Trade Book Set (27 books)	MMBS30

Grade 4

Complete Classroom Package   MMGS40

Contents: Teacher's Manual (2 volumes), Orientation Handbook and videos, Class Set (30 Student Books, Assessment Record Book), 27 trade books

Available separately

Classroom Materials without Trade Books	MMTP40
Teacher's Manual, vol. 1	MMTM40
Teacher's Manual, vol. 2	MMTM41
Replacement Class Set (30/1)	MMCS40
Student Book Pack (5 books)	MMSS40
Assessment Record Book	MMAB40
Trade Book Set (27 books)	MMBS40

Grade 5

Complete Classroom Package   MMGS50

Contents: Teacher's Manual (2 volumes), Orientation Handbook and videos, Class Set (30 Student Books, Assessment Record Book), 21 trade books

Available separately

Classroom Materials without Trade Books	MMTP50
Teacher's Manual, vol. 1	MMTM50
Teacher's Manual, vol. 2	MMTM51
Replacement Class Set (30/1)	MMCS50
Student Book Pack (5 books)	MMSS50
Assessment Record Book	MMAB50
Trade Book Set (21 books)	MMBS50

Grade 6

Complete Classroom Package   MMGS60

Contents: Teacher's Manual (2 volumes), Orientation Handbook and videos, Class Set (30 Student Books, Assessment Record Book), 20 trade books

Available separately

Classroom Materials without Trade Books	MMTP60
Teacher's Manual, vol. 1	MMTM60
Teacher's Manual, vol. 2	MMTM61
Replacement Class Set (30/1)	MMCS60
Student Book Pack (5 books)	MMSS60
Assessment Record Book	MMAB60
Trade Book Set (20 books)	MMBS60

Ordering Information:

To order call 800.666.7270 ∗ fax 510.842.0348
log on to www.devstu.org ∗ e-mail pubs@devstu.org

Or Mail Your Order to:

Developmental Studies Center ∗ Publications Department
2000 Embarcadero, Suite 305 ∗ Oakland, CA 94606

DEVELOPMENTAL
STUDIES CENTER™